MW00761791

Lord, Teach Us to Pray

How the Lord's Prayer Teaches Us to Pray

Robert C. McQuilkin

Columbia International University

Columbia, South Carolina

Lord, Teach Us to Pray: How the Lord's Prayer Teaches Us to Pray

Updated edition
Copyright © 2015 by Columbia International University

7435 Monticello Rd.
Columbia, SC 29203
www.ciu.edu

Columbia International University exists to train men and women from a
biblical worldview to impact the nations with the message of Christ through
service in the marketplace, missions and the local church.

Editing, Cover and interior book design by Kelly Smith, Tallgrass Media.
Cover photo from pixabay.com, Creative Commons Public Domain license.

Scripture quotations are from The Holy Bible, English Standard Version®
(ESV®), copyright © 2001 by Crossway, a publishing ministry of Good News
Publishers. Used by permission. All rights reserved.

No part of this book may be reproduced in any form or by any electronic
or mechanical means including information storage and retrieval systems,
without permission in writing from the publisher. The only exception is for
short excerpts quoted in a book review.

First Printing: 1943

ISBN-13: 978-1-939074-04-1

Contents

Introduction to the Series

Dr. Robert C. McQuilkin served as the first president of Columbia International University, then named Columbia Bible College (CBC) for 29 years; 1923-1952. He served Christ and the Church as a magazine editor, a dynamic speaker, and a prolific writer. But he also had a deep passion to teach. During his tenure as president, he taught Romans, John, Daniel and Revelation, Progress of Doctrine, Hermeneutics and other courses. The books in this series spilled over from those courses and from popular sermons he preached across the nation.

Dr. McQuilkin expressed the vision for a biblical university that outlines my own service as president: "Neither a Bible institute nor a liberal arts college, Columbia Bible College offers a curriculum with the spiritual advantages of the former, and the cultural advantages of the latter."

After Dr. McQuilkin's sudden death, G. Allen Fleece led the school in its move to CIU's present location. His plans for expansion laid the foundation for Dr. McQuilkin's son, Robertson, who became president in 1968 when Dr. Fleece returned to his first love of evangelism.

Robertson McQuilkin left the church planting work he loved in Japan to lead CIU from 1968 to 1990. Robertson, like his dad, writes, preaches, and teaches. His books on hermeneutics, world evangelization, ethics, and the Holy Spirit continue in print and are used by schools and ministries around the world.

I invite you to join us in revisiting our rich heritage of the written works of Robert and Robertson McQuilkin. After all, together they provided leadership to CIU for over 50 years.

Within their writings, you will notice themes that form CIU's core values:

- Biblical Authority: The authority of Scripture as the defining rule for belief and practice.
- Victorious Christian Life: The victory in Christ that every Christian can experience through the filling of the Spirit.
- Prayer and Faith: The consistent practice by every Christian of personal witness to God's saving work in Christ.
- World Evangelization: The alignment of every Christian with God's heart for those around the world who have never heard the gospel.
- Evangelical Unity: Protecting the core truths of the faith, while seeking evangelical unity on all nonessentials.

We still live by these five core values as a school and to revisit them again in these books solidifies our commitment to them. We look back to remember and to underscore the importance of remaining tethered to our foundations, while exercising relevance in a dynamic, global community.

We look forward, until Christ returns, to serving His church by educating people from a biblical worldview to impact the nations with the message of Christ.

Dr. Bill Jones
President, Columbia International University
www.ciu.edu

Foreword

Why re-publish the writings of one who died more than a half century ago? Well, some would say, because they are classics by a major Christian author. But there's more.

Ninety years after their founding, very few institutions accurately reflect all the core values the founder held. But the grace of God through the creative genius of my father, Robert C. McQuilkin, has done just that. He was involved with initiating many movements and institutions. Some have morphed into something different than he envisioned. Some have disappeared. But the institution he poured his life into — Columbia Bible College — continues to this day in the vision and path he laid down, known today as Columbia International University.

Perhaps the enduring impact of his writing results in part, not only for its biblical fidelity on the God-intended life, but because his writing was signed and sealed by the life of the author. As I testified at his memorial service in 1952, "I know my father has sinned because 'all have sinned.' But I want you to know that for 25 years living in his house, I've never known him to fail."

It is fitting that this treasure trove should once again be made available to the CIU family and, as in the beginning, far beyond.

J. Robertson McQuilkin
President Emeritus
Columbia International University

Photo of Robertson McQuilkin with his father in the 1950s.

The Lord's Prayer

Matthew 6:9-14

English Standard Version (ESV)

Pray then like this:

Our Father in heaven,
hallowed be your name.
Your kingdom come,
your will be done,
    on earth as it is in heaven.
Give us this day our daily bread,
and forgive us our debts,
    as we also have forgiven our debtors.
And lead us not into temptation,
but deliver us from evil.

[For yours is the Kingdom, and the power,
    and the glory, forever. Amen.]

Chapter 1

"Lord, Make Me a Man of Prayer"

S ome years ago I had the privilege of conducting my first Bible and missionary conference in the church of the sainted Dr. Joseph Kelly of Washington, D.C. The most vivid recollection of that happy week spent in the home of Dr. and Mrs. Kelly, both now with the Lord, was the parting word of this dear Christian woman, who seemed to me to be as near to God as anyone I had ever met. "When you think of me," she said, "I want you to ask just one thing from the Lord. Ask him to make me a woman of prayer. I am not."

Many times in the past years have I thought of this request. I questioned her judgment of herself when she said, "I am not." But I must confess that when I thought of Mrs. Kelly, my prayer was, "Lord, make me a man of prayer."

To be a man or woman of prayer is to solve all problems of life. To pray aright is to live aright. Not that prayer is a substitute for doing anything else that needs to be done. But true prayer will make possible the doing of everything that needs to be done, in the most effective and victorious way.

Our Lord Jesus Christ himself was a man of prayer. Indeed, He was the only One who lived a perfect prayer life. Our aim, but not our attainment, is to become like Jesus in our prayer life. Nevertheless, in our own measure and degree we may be men and women of prayer, in a sense in which most Christians are not.

"Now Jesus was praying in a certain place, and when he finished, one of his disciples said to him, 'Lord, teach us to pray, as John taught his disciples'" (Luke 11:1).

This request of the disciple, "Lord, teach us to pray," was prompted by the example of the Master's own praying, and by the remembrance that John the Baptist had taught his disciples how to pray. There must have been an immeasurable difference between the simple prayer suggestions given by John the Baptist, or perhaps the form of prayer he gave, and the communion of the Lord Jesus Christ with his Father. So also there is a wide difference between what was in the mind of this disciple who said, "Lord, teach us to pray", and the instruction the Lord gave them, both at this time, and in his farewell message, and later through the Holy Spirit.

The Lord's immediate answer to this request was, as in all cases, altogether worthy of him. No other man spoke like this man; no other man taught as he taught. His teachings to the disciples were simple, clear and elementary. They could make use of the truth at once. And yet those teachings included the germ of all the truth that yet was to be unfolded by the Holy Spirit, speaking through the writers of the New Testament.

Our Lord's immediate answer to the question was to give them what we call the Lord's Prayer. Already the Lord had given this prayer in the Sermon on the Mount, which came during the first part of his Galilean ministry. In this passage in Luke, our Lord had finished the Galilean ministry and was facing toward Jerusalem, just a few months before his crucifixion. In both cases, however, the Lord's Prayer was given as instruction to his disciples on how to pray. It is not given primarily for the purpose of repeating the words, although it was inevitable that his followers should use these precious words in approaching the Father. Here in Luke, in our English translation, we have fifty-six words (not including the doxology), and in the fifty-six words the Lord is teaching the great principles of prayer; perhaps no other equal portion of Scripture is more filled with meaning.

Chapter 2

The Approach To Prayer

Before we ask these rich words of the Lord's Prayer to unfold their meaning to us on how to pray, let us notice first the approach to prayer. What should be our attitude before we enter into prayer? It is true that the opening words, "Our Father in heaven," suggest the approach. But it is interesting that the five closing verses of the tenth chapter of Luke, just preceding the disciples' request to teach them to pray, gives a striking message on our approach to prayer.

One of the exquisite glimpses the Gospel gives us into the personal life of the Lord Jesus is his visit to the home of Martha and Mary. Martha is in charge of the house. She receives the Lord. We see Mary sitting at Jesus' feet. We see Martha "distracted with much serving." We hear her complaint, "Lord, do you not care that my sister has left me to serve alone? Tell her then to help me." Then follows the gentle rebuke, "Martha, Martha, you are anxious and troubled about many things, but one thing is necessary. Mary has chosen the good portion, which will not be taken away from her."

Very often this passage is treated as presenting to us two Christians with different characteristics, Martha, the active, busy Christian; Mary, the thoughtful, meditative believer. But this is to miss the whole point of the narrative. It is quite true that Christians do have different characteristics. It also seems evident that Martha was one who was busy and active. She was much like Peter in some ways. We remember also that Martha witnessed to her faith in the Lord in almost the same words as Peter's great confession: "Yes, Lord; I believe that you are the Christ, the Son of God, who is coming into the world" (John 11:27).

Mary has often been pictured as a rather impractical woman who would not be much use in housework, or in getting a meal. If that were the case, we wonder why Martha was so disturbed that her sister was not helping her; it would be a relief for her to have her sister away so that she might prepare the meal unhindered.

But the point of this passage is a contrast, not between the two different kinds of believers, but between two earnest, beloved believers, one of whom was anxious and troubled, and the other committing herself wholly to the presence and the teaching of the Lord. We must remember that the Lord Jesus rebuked Martha, and commended Mary. We need to inquire as to why Martha was rebuked, and why Mary was commended. There may be truth in the saying, "We need both Marthas and Marys in the church." But we do not need Marthas and Marys in the sense in which Martha was defeated and Mary was victorious. There is no doubt that Martha received the rebuke of the Lord, and that her attitude was changed by it. So in this sense the Lord wants every Christian to take the attitude that Mary took. What was that attitude?

Mary had chosen the good part. She had the one thing that was needful. What is that one thing? Occupation with Christ, and complete trust in him.

Three times Mary appears before us in the Gospel. On each occasion she is at the feet of Jesus. Here she is at the feet of Jesus hearing his word. When her brother Lazarus is dead, she is at the feet of Jesus in sorrow, trusting him for comfort and deliverance. In the scene before his death, she is at the feet of Jesus in adoring love, pouring out the alabaster box of precious ointment.

While each Christian expresses devotion to the Lord in different ways, the attitude of Mary's heart is to be the attitude of every trusting child of God. We have here two devoted believers in the Lord equally rich in his love: "Now Jesus loved Martha and Mary and Lazarus." That was the most wonderful thing about these two sisters and brother: Jesus loved them. That is the greatest possession that each of us has; but do we always trust that love? Are we always counting upon it? Perfect love casts out fear. Christ's perfect love toward us casts out all fear. Do we not have to confess that often we have been like Martha, "anxious and troubled"?

Martha was anxious, Mary was abiding; Martha was troubled, Mary, trusting; Martha complaining, Mary contented; Martha restless, Mary resting; Martha care-full, Mary care-free; Martha worried, Mary worshiping; Martha disturbed, Mary devoted; Martha jealous, Mary joyful; Martha fretful, Mary fervent; Martha grumbling, Mary gracious; Martha defeated, Mary delivered; and so the contrasts might be summed up: Martha was occupied with self, Mary was occupied with Christ.

These words describe not only Martha and Mary, on this particular occasion, but our own experience at the time when we are not trusting the Lord, and at the time when we are realizing that one thing is needful and we have chosen the good part.

But what has this to do with prayer? It is true that this incident has no immediate historical connection with what follows in the eleventh chapter of Luke. Nevertheless, there is a vital logical connection. Mary's attitude before the Lord is the true approach to prayer.

The glorious passage on prayer in Philippians 4:6, 7 illustrates this connection: "do not be anxious about anything, but in everything by prayer and supplication with thanksgiving let your requests be made known to God. And the peace of God, which surpasses all understanding, will guard your hearts and your minds in Christ Jesus."

Here we have the approach to prayer: "Do not be anxious about anything." This does not mean that there are not many things to bring anxiety to a Christian. It does mean that prayer is the cure for care. We may come with great burdens on our heart, but we come "not anxious about anything," that is, assured of the solution of the problem that is troubling us. This was the attitude of Mary, sitting at the feet of the Lord Jesus to hear his words. She could not have anxiety because in Christ every anxiety would be cared for. Nevertheless, they had to be brought to him.

Following this approach to prayer, we have, in the passage in Luke, the teaching on how to pray. Then there follows the result of prayer. So also in the Philippian passage, after the description of how to pray, we have the result: "And the peace of God, which surpasses all understanding, will guard your hearts and your minds in Christ Jesus."

Chapter 3

The Father and his Child

No other portion of Scripture, not even the twenty-third Psalm, has been repeated so often, and is known by so many people as the Lord's Prayer. But like the twenty-third Psalm, we may know the words of this prayer without entering into the marvels of its message.

The Lord gave it not primarily as a prayer to be prayed by great congregations, nor for ritual use, but in answer to the request, "Lord, teach us to pray." There is no doubt that God is pleased when his people pray these words in the Spirit. But when large companies of people repeat the Lord's Prayer there is the danger that unbelievers will pray, "Our Father," and be encouraged to count themselves children of God without meeting the conditions.

There are teachers who claim that the Lord's Prayer is not intended for Christians, but rather for Jewish disciples before the death and resurrection of Christ, or for Jewish believers in a future age. It is to be regretted that such a wrong understanding of the Lord's Prayer should turn Christians aside from one of the most marvelous passages in the New Testament, and one which is intended to teach us the secret of prevailing prayer.

The fact is that this prayer is intended only for believers. None others except children of God can pray the Lord's Prayer. This brings us to the first teaching, found in the address of the prayer: "Our Father in heaven."

Here we are faced with the simplest secret of prayer, and the most profound. God is our Father, and we come in prayer as children to the Father in heaven. Notice this relationship. There is the relationship of God to the one who is praying. There is also the relationship of the believer with all other believers expressed in "our" Father. In this relationship of Father and children there is the basis for all prayer.

In our Lord's farewell message recorded in John 14, 15, 16, he speaks to them again and again about prayer. And always these prayer promises are linked with the fact that the love of the Father and of the Son for these disciples, and their love for the Father and the Son, is the basis of the prayer relationship. The ground of the Lord's prayer, as of all others is, of course, the blood of Christ. It is because of the Father's love that Christ was sent to die for our sins. It is because of his death and resurrection that he is able to send the Holy Spirit who comes to abide in our heart and to make intercession for us.

Our Lord, in speaking of the new knowledge of prayer that they will have after his death and resurrection, says: "In that day you will ask in my name, and I do not say to you that I will ask the Father on your behalf; for the Father himself loves you, because you have loved me and have believed that I came from God" (John 16:26, 27). The love of God the Father for his Son, the Lord Jesus Christ, is evident in what the Father gives him in answer to prayer: "The Father loves the Son and has given all things into his hand" (John 3:35). We are in Christ, and we come in the name of Christ. It is only through him that we are able to say, "Our Father." Thus we begin our prayer with the consciousness that he is our Father, and we are his children.

We may conclude then that the first lesson in prayer is that we should come with absolute assurance of our salvation. When we take Christ as our own personal Saviour, we are born of the Spirit and thus we become children of God. Because we are his children, God has sent forth the Spirit of his Son into our hearts, crying "Abba, Father." This we call the "witness of the Spirit." We read in Romans 8:16, "The Spirit himself bears witness with our spirit that we are children of God." Every Christian has the witness of the Spirit that they are a child of God. However, there are Christians who are troubled about the assurance of salvation.

Notice that the Word does not say, "The Spirit bears witness *to* our spirit," but "*with* our spirit." The thought is that the Holy Spirit is the Spirit of God the Son. He is the Spirit of Christ, as well as the Spirit of God the Father. The theologians express this by saying that the Holy Spirit proceeds from the Father and also from the Son. So when we are born of the Spirit, the Holy Spirit comes into our heart, and the Holy Spirit says, "Father; "then our spirits say, "Father."

There are three witnesses to our salvation: the witness of the Word, the witness of the Spirit, the witness of the life. We would never know that Christ died for our sins if it were not for the revelation of God's Word. We would not know that when we repent and believe we are born of the Spirit, apart from the Word of God. Therefore, the assurance of our salvation must always rest upon the Word of God. How blessedly simple he has made it. If we are really convicted of our sins, and know that we are sinners, and that Christ, the Son of God, died for us, then the choice is definite and simple. "Whoever believes in the Son has eternal life; whoever does not obey the Son shall not see life, but the wrath of God remains on him." Here we have two classes only: those who believe, and those who do not believe. Which class are you in? I make my choice at this moment as to which class I belong in. If I believe in him, then I know that I have eternal life, because God has declared this in his Word.

There is the possibility that a man may say that he believes without really believing. If a man says he has faith, but has not works, "can that faith save him?" (James 2:14.) The answer is, "No, that faith cannot save him," just because it is not faith. The man either has not repented, or has not really believed that Christ, the Son of God, died on the cross for his sins. For if a man believes that, he is born of the Spirit (1 John 5:1)

Following the witness of the Word, is the witness of the Spirit. When I make a decision to repent of my sin, and to trust Christ for salvation, then I have the witness of the Spirit that I am a child of God. This does not refer to any particular feeling. It is rather the consciousness, or the knowledge, that God is my Father and that I am his child. With one believer this may result in an overwhelming emotion. With another there may be a quiet peace in the assurance. With others there may be a struggle with doubt, and the feeling of assurance may be lacking.

My dear friend L. L. Legters, who was used to lead many to Christ, one time spoke of the men he had prayed with who had not been brought up in Christian homes and were not accustomed to pray. He said that in every case such men started their prayer, "O God." But in every case when a man took Christ as his Saviour, without being conscious that he was doing it, he addressed God as "Father."

I quoted Mr. Legters on this at a Bible conference. There was a young woman present who had been brought up in a non-believing home, knowing nothing of the Bible or prayer before her salvation. The first prayer of this young woman had been the prayer, "O God, if you are alive, reveal yourself to me." She came up at the close of the meeting with a glowing face and said, "That was just my experience. After I took Christ as my Saviour, without knowing I was doing it, I found myself praying to God as my Father." That is an expression of the witness of the Spirit.

But to come back to this question of the believer who does not have assurance. If someone should ask you whether you knew you were saved, perhaps you would say, "I wish I were sure." And yet is it not true that when you pray you do not hesitate to say, "Our Father"? If there is lack of assurance, should we not pray this way: "Father, if you are my Father, and if I am Your child, I do want to bring my needs to You. I am not sure I am Your child, but in case I am, I want to pray to You. I want to bring my burdens to You, in case You are my Father."

We can see at once that this would not be a good basis for getting satisfaction in our prayers. Our Lord wants us to be definite in prayer. The first thing to be definite about is that God is my Father, and I am his child.

But our Lord started the prayer, "Our Father," not "My Father." When we take Christ as our Saviour, we are joined to God in Christ. Union with Christ is indeed the essence of our salvation; but when we take Christ as our Saviour we are baptized by the Holy Spirit into the Body of Christ, There is not only that personal, individual relationship with Christ; there is also union with all other believers. He is "Our Father," and there is in our prayers the sense of our union with all other members of the family. This does not mean that it would be wrong to address God as "My Father." It does mean that our Lord is teaching us how to pray. Not only when we pray together, but when we enter into closets, the One we address is "Our Father."

Along with the certainty and assurance that is expressed in the word "Father," there is also the close, intimate fellowship suggested in this relationship. The words follow, "in heaven." We come before God with reverence and awe, because he is the mighty God. He is in heaven; we are on earth. How blessedly are these two great truths revealed in our address in prayer. He is "Father," the word that suggests tender and intimate fellowship. Many are the stories of sons who have entered into the presence of great men, kings and presidents and generals, when none other would dare to enter. But linked with this is the other truth that we are in the presence of the mighty God.

Have we learned this lesson? There are two common mistakes in the approach that Christians make to God because of failure to learn these lessons: the lesson contained in the word "Father," and the lesson contained in the word "in heaven."

Many Christians, especially those of an older generation, are accustomed to avoid the use of the name God both in public and in private prayer. He is called "The Almighty," and sometimes in more colloquial language he is referred to as "The Good Man," or "The Good Man in heaven." The Jews avoided writing out the name of Jehovah, and even today the scholars are not certain as to how the name of the covenant God was pronounced. Jewish rabbis today will not write out the name God, but will write G-d, with the thought that if the paper should fall to the ground someone might put his foot on the name of God.

We can honor the reverent thought in such views, but as a practical matter it has meant that many Christians have felt far off from God. They have not learned the meaning of "Father."

Today we are in danger of an opposite error. There is often too great familiarity in the use of the name of the Lord. This familiarity may become almost flippant. Sometimes there is an unconscious nervous habit in prayer of repeating the name of the Lord in one form or another in practically every sentence. This is a careless use of the holy name of God. There is among young Christians the danger of being too free and even irreverent in the use of the Lord's name both in conversation and in prayer.

When we pray in the Spirit we may have the full benefit of the tender, intimate familiar relationship that the word "Father" teaches us, and also the reverent awe in the consciousness that God is in heaven and we are on earth; he is the creator and we are the creatures: "Our Father in heaven."

Chapter 4

Hallowed Be Your Name

If we have learned the lesson thus far in Christ's school of prayer, we are coming to him in the right attitude of prayer, because of our faith and confidence in him, because of our certainty that prayer will not be in vain; we have come with assurance that he is our Father, and that we are his children; thus we are coming with reverent awe, and yet with boldness and confidence to the throne of grace to obtain mercy and to find grace to help in time of need (Hebrews 4:16). He has told us to come, and to pour out our heart before him (Psalm 62:8).

Now, how shall we begin our prayer? Shall we tell the Father of our own sins, and how we have disappointed him? Shall we tell him that we are unworthy to come into his presence? Shall we ask him to convict us of sin that we may have our sins cleansed, and be prepared to pray? These might be natural things on the heart of any Christian as he or she begins to pray.

However, if we come with a heart burdened for some loved one who is ill, or more greatly burdened for some loved one who is away from God, do we not naturally first pour out our heart before God for them?

Perhaps we come to the Lord greatly burdened with problems that we do not know how to solve. These problems are possessing our thoughts. We can give attention to nothing until we have some light upon them. So we come to our Father and bring them urgently before him.

Perhaps we are in great sorrow. A loved one has died. We come to the Father to pour out our heart before him. There may be a temptation to resent the fact that the Lord did not spare the life, or there may be an overwhelming sense of loneliness, and we come to God for comfort.

But if we should come to the Lord in prayer and speak first of our own sins, our own unworthiness, our own sorrow, our own problems, the spiritual needs of ourselves or our loved ones, we are beginning the prayer with self. And that is not the way to begin our prayers.

The Lord has taught us how to pray. He has given us the first petitions for our prayer; "Hallowed be Your name. Your kingdom come. Your will be done in earth, as it is in heaven." It is *your* name, *your* kingdom, *your* will. The chief end of man is to glorify God. The beginning of every true prayer must be to glorify God. We are to be occupied with him, with his honor, with his kingdom, with his will.

Since our Father is in heaven and we on earth, we want his name to be hallowed here on earth as in heaven; we want his kingdom to come on earth as in heaven; we want his will to be done on earth as in heaven. This is the consummation of all our desires, is it not?

Here is a searching test for our prayers. We naturally are centered in ourselves. This does not mean that we are selfish, in the ordinary sense of that term. We may be convicted of our own sins, and our own unworthiness. In that sense we are centered upon ourselves. We may be praying for our loved ones who are sick, or pleading for loved ones who are out of Christ. In all of these things there is danger of thinking of them from the standpoint of self, and not from the standpoint of our Father.

Sometimes it is said that we should put Christ first, and our family second. But that is a mistake. We should put Christ first, and no one else should come second. When he is the supreme object of our worship and desire, all other things take their proper place. We shall learn how to pray for our loved ones primarily for his glory, and not primarily for our own comfort, or primarily for their good. What a wonderful secret to learn that the thing that is for God's glory is the thing that is for our best good.

The Shorter Westminster Catechism poses the question, "What do we pray for in the first petition?" The answer is: "In the first petition, which is, 'Hallowed be Your name', we pray that God would enable us, and others, to glorify him in all that whereby He maketh himself known, and that He would dispose all things to his own glory."

The name of God is the means of making himself known. When God is glorified, whether in the individual heart, or in the church, or in a home, or in a city, in the nation or in the world, then all else falls into its right place.

Many are asking why it is that the earth has been devastated by war during the two thousand years since the angels sang: "Peace on earth, good will to men." But that is not what the angels said. They said, "Glory to God in the highest, and on earth peace, good will to men." It is when God's name is hallowed that the blessing of peace, and every other blessing comes.

When we hallow the name of God, we not only honor him and exalt him for his greatness and his great goodness, but we trust him with full assurance of faith. For his name reveals all that he is to us.

The glory of God is revealed in his name. "his name shall be called Wonderful, Counselor, Mighty God, Everlasting Father, Prince of Peace" (Isaiah 9:6). T. C. Horton in his book, "That Wonderful Name," studies the names that were given to the Lord Jesus Christ, including the titles and descriptions. He includes three hundred and sixty-five names, one for every day in the year. Some have said that the Lord's

Prayer is not prayed in the name of Jesus. But the names of the Lord Jesus are the names of God. It is true that the disciples at that time did not realize the significance of asking in the name of Jesus, because it was through his death and resurrection and ascension to the right hand of power that they learned what it meant to pray in the name of Christ. Nevertheless, it is all included in this word, "Hallowed be Your name."

There is one Psalm, and only one, which is called "David's Psalm of Praise," the 145th. "I will extol You, my God and King; and will bless thy name forever and ever." This Psalm of praise goes on to give the reasons for praising the name of the Lord. It is because of his greatness, because of his mighty works to every generation, because of the glorious majesty of his honor, the might of his terrible acts, the memory of his great goodness, his righteousness, his grace and mercy, and loving kindness, his goodness to all, his tender mercies over all his works, the glory of his kingdom, his mighty power, his upholding of those that fall and raising up of those that are bowed down, his giving of food in due season and satisfying the desire of every living thing, his nearness to those that call upon him, his fulfilling the desire of those that fear him, his answering the prayer of those in need, his preserving all those that love him, his destruction of the wicked.

This is the beginning of true prayer, to be occupied with God, as revealed in Christ our Lord. He is the altogether lovely One, and his praise may continually fill our mouths. Those who have suggested there is no thanksgiving or praise in the Lord's Prayer have missed the meaning of "Hallowed be Your name."

It is natural that the petition: "Hallowed be Your name," should follow, "Our Father in heaven." We have spoken of the need of reverence in the use of God's name. In our day there is great danger of lightly using the name of the Lord because of the widespread growth of a pseudo religion. When we use the name of the Lord in a popular song like the song which swept over America, "Praise the Lord and Pass the Ammunition," we are certainly not hallowing the name of the Lord. We are taking the name of the Lord in vain. It is true that Christians who honor the name of the Lord may be the bravest of fighters, and the most efficient in passing the ammunition in battle, but the flippant use of the sacred name in a popular song is dragging the living God down to the level of our own light-hearted view of the world.

A noted surgeon who performed an operation on the writer made some of my friends glad by his evident piety, when he said we would have to trust the Lord for certain features of the recovery. I asked him later whether he really meant trust the Lord, or whether he was referring to the processes of nature. He hesitated a moment, and then said he supposed he was referring to nature. I asked him if he had thought of this as one way of taking the name of the Lord in vain. It had not occurred to him, although he was a church officer. Men who are thoroughly secular and who have no knowledge of the Lord Jesus often use his name as a respectful accommodation to the language used by Christians whom they may love and honor. All of this is far from hallowing the great and terrible name of the mighty God.

One of the ominous signs of the breakdown of moral and spiritual standards in America is the growth of profane swearing. George Washington was concerned in his day about the growth of this habit, and in an order to his army asked how they could expect God's blessing if his name were constantly blasphemed. But today it is not merely the careless and thoughtless use of God's name by the vulgar and ignorant, by the drunkards and immoral. It is the widespread use of profanity in our literature, among society leaders and cultured people, in high school and college, in the armed forces, in business and industry, in politics and even among our national leaders, — it is this that should warn us of the growing apostasy and approaching judgment. When God's name and God's way and God's book are lightly regarded in America, we may well tremble for our land. When we pray or sing "God Bless America," if we are not taking his name in vain, we are praying for conviction of sin and a turning back to God in repentance.

This petition, "Hallowed be Your name," prayed many millions of times, will be answered in a final overwhelming manner, and one day that great name will be hallowed by every creature. Every knee will bow to Christ, even though many will not bow as saved souls.

Chapter 5

Your Kingdom Come

In the first petition we are occupied especially with the person of our God. In the second petition, the thought turns toward his mighty works and his plans for the children of men: "Your kingdom come."

In Psalm 145, David cries out in praise: "All your works shall give thanks to you, O Lord, and all your saints shall bless you! They shall speak of the glory of your kingdom and tell of your power, to make known to the children of man your mighty deeds, and the glorious splendor of your kingdom. Your kingdom is an everlasting kingdom, and your dominion endures throughout all generations" (Psalm 145:10-13.)

For what are we asking when we pray, "Your kingdom come"? There are several different stages in the manifestation of God's kingdom on earth. In the Old Testament, beginning with the call of Abraham, God's kingdom was committed to Israel. The greatest glory of that kingdom was under David and Solomon. Israel was never called to be an end in herself. Abraham was called to be a blessing to all nations of the earth. To that end the name Abram, exalted father, was changed to Abraham, "father of many nations." The mission of Israel was to make known to all nations on earth the true God whose name was revealed to them. When Israel rejected Christ, she rejected God her King. When the Lord gave to the leaders of the Jews that terrible parable of the husbandman who killed the servants, and then killed the only, well-beloved son of the owner of the vineyard, He spoke to them these solemn words: "Therefore I tell you, the kingdom of God will be taken away from you and given to a people producing its fruits" (Matt. 21:43).

Today we have that new manifestation of the kingdom of God on earth. Our Lord took the kingdom away from the nation of Israel, and gave it to a new body, the Church, composed of Jews and Gentiles, here figuratively called a "nation." In this same way Peter speaks, "But you are a chosen race, a royal priesthood, a holy nation, a people for his own possession, that you may proclaim the excellencies of him who called you out of darkness into his marvelous light. Once you were not a people, but now you are God's people; once you had not received mercy, but now you have received mercy" (1 Pet. 2:9, 10). Our Lord taught that the key to the entering of this Kingdom is the new birth: "Unless one is born again, he cannot see the kingdom of God." So when we pray, "Your kingdom come," we are praying for souls to be born into the Kingdom today. We are praying that the Gospel may go to the uttermost part of the earth. The prayer should give us a passion for sharing the Good News of Christ, and for foreign missions.

But it is very evident in this petition that there is to be a future manifestation of the Kingdom. Some speak of the present Kingdom of grace, and the future Kingdom of glory. The Kingdom is a Kingdom of grace from beginning to end. It is a Kingdom of glory from beginning to end, although we look forward to the final consummation when all things shall be put under our Lord Jesus.

When our Lord drew near to Jerusalem, where he knew he would be crucified, his disciples were looking forward to a crown of glory, not to a crown of thorns. They evidently expected that Christ would be received as Messiah, that by his mighty power he would overcome all opposition, and they would reign with him in the Kingdom that was to be set up. This is plainly stated in Luke 19:11, "As they heard these things, he proceeded to tell a parable, because he was near to Jerusalem, and because they supposed that the kingdom of God was to appear immediately." This is a clear statement by the Spirit of God that the Kingdom of God was not immediately to appear. The parable that our Lord gave of the nobleman that went into a far country to receive for himself a kingdom and to return, plainly refers to the fact that the Lord Jesus was to go to his Father and receive the Kingdom and then was to return to reward his servants and to punish his enemies. When we pray, "Your Kingdom Come," we are praying that the Lord Jesus Christ may come back to this earth to reign. The last prayer in the Bible, "Even so, come, Lord Jesus," is an echo of this petition, "Your kingdom come."

In that marvelous second Psalm, God the Father is speaking to the Son: "Ask of me, and I will make the nations your heritage, and the ends of the earth your possession" (Psalm 2:8). When we pray that the Gospel might go to the ends of the earth, and that Christ might come to reign and break down the power of the enemy, we are praying with the Lord Jesus. In the seventy-second Psalm it is written, "May prayer be made for him continually, and blessings invoked for him all the day!" When we pray, "Your kingdom come," we are looking forward also to the final consummation.

The Scriptures indicate that the next manifestation of the Kingdom will be during that thousand years when we shall reign with Christ over the nations of the earth, when the nations of the earth shall have beat their swords into plowshares and their spears into pruning-hooks. This is the time when the Kingdom is restored to Israel. When the disciples said, "Lord, will you at this time restore the kingdom to Israel?" they were not speaking out of their ignorance. For forty days

the Lord had been appearing to them and speaking the things concerning the Kingdom of God (Acts 1:3). They knew that he had taken
the Kingdom away from Israel (Matt. 21:43). They are asking about
the time when the Kingdom would be restored. Just as the Church of
Christ is now entrusted with the Kingdom, and entrusted with the
responsibility of taking the Gospel to the uttermost part of the earth,
so in this coming age the Kingdom will be restored to Israel. This does
not mean a "carnal" kingdom. It means that for the first time there will
be a nation that will glorify the Lord Jesus Christ. God's purpose for
Israel will be carried out. His purpose was to bless all nations through
Israel. Israel was never to be an end in herself, but always a means to
the end. As at the beginning of this age the Gospel went to the Jew
first, and through the remnant of the Jews who accepted Christ the
blessing will go to all the nations of the earth through restored Israel.
Paul cries in exultation that if the fall of Israel meant the riches of the
Gentiles, what will the fullness of Israel be; that is, what will happen
when not a remnant but all Israel accepts Christ; he cannot put it into
words and he calls it, "Life from the dead" (Rom. 11:12). This we pray
for when we pray, "Your kingdom come."

Yet at the close of this thousand-year period of universal peace
and prevailing righteousness, there is permitted a final revolt under
Satan. Then comes the destruction of the heaven and the earth and
the creation of the new heaven and the new earth, and God rules over
all. At that time the Son turns the Kingdom over to the Father: "Then
comes the end, when he delivers the kingdom to God the Father after
destroying every rule and every authority and power. For he must reign
until he has put all his enemies under his feet. The last enemy to be
destroyed is death" (1 Cor. 15:24-26).

Many teach that when Christ returns there will be no reign of a thousand years, but that the earth will at that time be destroyed and the new heaven and new earth will be created. But at Christ's coming, the Father gives the Son the Kingdom (Luke 19:12; Dan. 7:14); the kingdoms of this world become the kingdoms of Christ (Rev. 11:15). At the final consummation the Son delivers up the Kingdom to the Father.

How rich is the content of that prayer, "Your Kingdom come." Let us ever associate the Kingdom with the King; when Paul preached the Kingdom of God it meant the preaching of the things concerning Jesus (Acts 28:23, 31). When we long for the coming of the Kingdom we are looking for that blessed Hope, the glorious appearing of our God and Saviour Jesus Christ (Titus 2:13). When we labor for that Kingdom we are hastening his coming, for the one thing he commanded his Church to do was to take the Gospel to the ends of the earth. (Acts 1:8)

If we would pray after this manner, "Your Kingdom come," we must become intercessors for the salvation of souls about us and also missionary intercessors. The prayer letters of missionaries, the magazines and books that make the missionary needs known should be fuel for our urgent prayers. Let us not forget the hundreds of millions who have never heard the Gospel. The world is open as never before to take the Gospel to every unreached land. And this great new opportunity is in answer to the prayer, "Your Kingdom Come."

Chapter 6

Your Will Be Done

In the first petition we are occupied especially with the person of our God. In the second petition, the thought turns toward his mighty works and his plans for the children of men: "Your kingdom come."

The last of the three petitions that are linked together in the opening of our prayer and praise, is: "Your will be done in earth, as it is in heaven." This petition is vitally linked to the petitions concerning the hallowing of God's name and the coming of his Kingdom. The prayer may well be read: "Hallowed be Your name, in earth as it is in heaven; Your kingdom come on earth, as it is in heaven; Your will be done in earth, as it is in heaven." In any case, when the will of God is done in earth as it is in heaven, then will his name be hallowed perfectly, as the angels hallow it in heaven, and then will his Kingdom be present on the earth.

The glory of heaven is the fact that the will of God is done there. The glory of any life here on earth is to do the will of God. When we pray, "Your will be done," we are praying that the Holy Spirit might control our lives here and now.

In the first eleven chapters of Romans the Holy Spirit presents through Paul the wonders of God's plan of redemption in saving men by grace through faith. Then in view of this marvelous thing that God has done for these Christians, Paul in the Spirit writes: "I appeal to you therefore, brothers, by the mercies of God, to present your bodies as a living sacrifice, holy and acceptable to God, which is your spiritual worship." Then he goes on to explain the meaning of this life that is fully surrendered to the control of the Spirit of God: "Do not be conformed to this world, but be transformed by the renewal of your mind, that by testing you may discern what is the will of God, what is good and acceptable and perfect." This is what follows the surrender of the life to Christ. We enter into the will of God. In the measure in which we live in this will of God here on earth, we have a foretaste of heaven on earth.

Some have suggested that God has a perfect will for every Christian. If the Christian misses that perfect will, there is a second-best will, which may be called acceptable. Again, if we miss the acceptable will of God, there is a "good" will of God. But this is to miss the meaning of the will of God. God's will is the one good thing, the best thing for God's glory and for the Christian's good; it is "that good part" which Mary chose. This will of God is described as being "good." It is not a matter of comparison, as though there was something good, and something else still better. Then this will of God is described as acceptable, or well pleasing, or as the word literally suggests, delightful. The will of God is well pleasing to God; it is well pleasing to us. Finally, this will is described as "perfect." This word gives the thought of finality. It is the final thing. Blessed will of God, this is the one place of rest in time and in eternity.

Now when the will of God is presented to us, we receive it or we reject it. We do not choose a second-best will, because God does not offer a second-best will to any man. Here is a Christian who in his younger days was called to go to the ministry or to the mission field, and turned away from the plan of God. In a sense, he may speak of having chosen God's second-best plan for his life. But this is not the case. He rejected God's will. When he comes to see his failure in disobedience, God forgives that sin and now deals with him as he is and where he is. God now has a perfect will for his life in the present situation where he is, though it is not that original plan. God can restore the years that the locusts have eaten, for where sin abounds, grace does much more abound.

When there is trouble in any individual life, it is because the will of God is not being done. So if there is trouble in the family, in the Church, in the school, in the nation, that trouble is because the will of God is not being fulfilled. It is the will of God that Christ should have preeminence in all things. Today he is not given preeminence in the political world, so inevitably we have war and confusion. To the extent that Christ is honored to that extent will there be blessings upon the nations. In the degree in which Christ is not given the preeminence, in that degree will trouble and judgment come. In Christ are hid all the treasures of wisdom and knowledge. To the extent that Christ is given the preeminence in the educational world, there is blessing. But confusion and darkness is resulting because the world of education is leaving Christ out. They are seeking to have the fruits of freedom without the root.

It is the will of God that Christ should have the preeminence in his Church. He is the head of the Church. To the extent that Christ is given this place of preeminence, to that extent there is blessing. And so the trouble and divisions in the local church, or in a denomination, is due to the fact that Christ is not given the preeminence. He has preeminence in salvation. When we exalt Christ, and yield to his control, we are doing the will of God.

When we pray, "Your will be done in earth, as it is in heaven," is there to be a future, complete fulfillment of this petition? Christian believers today are distressed, and doubtless our distress should be deeper and more poignant, because the will of God is not being done. There is the dishonoring of God's name, God's book, God's day, God's church, and God's Gospel. But there is the promise that one day every knee shall bow, and all the earth shall honor and hallow the name of the Lord Jesus Christ our God. The Kingdom of God will come on the earth, and the will of God shall be carried out on earth as it is in heaven.

How significant is it today that even Christian kings and rulers of earth, when they speak of God, intending to do him honor, carefully omit the name of the Lord Jesus Christ. On Christmas day in 1942, the King of England, a true child of God, who with his wife, confesses and honors Christ as his Saviour, gave a wartime Christmas message to the Empire, broadcast to the world, and he spoke of Almighty God but made no reference to the name of the Lord Jesus. Yet Christ's birthday was the occasion of the message, and Great Britain is officially Christian. The President of the United States, when he speaks, does not honor the name of the Lord Jesus Christ, feeling that officially he cannot do so, since the United States is not officially Christian. One day we will look back with regret that the name of Christ was not honored. O that kings and rulers might hear and heed the Word of God in the second Psalm: "Now therefore, O kings, be wise; be warned, O rulers of the earth. Serve the Lord with fear, and rejoice with trembling. Kiss the Son, lest he be angry, and you perish in the way, for his wrath is quickly kindled. Blessed are all who take refuge in him" (Psa. 2:10-12).

When we hear that Satan's kingdom is progressing, and that many are turning away from the Lord, and that God's Kingdom is not coming, then we may rejoice that these petitions *will* be answered, and that we have the joy and certainty that his Kingdom *will* come. When we see in all the world that the will of Christ is not sought, but rather the will of man, we remember that the Holy Spirit predicted clearly that in the last days men should be lovers of self and should follow all the sins that go with this, and worst of all, they would be "having the appearance of godliness, but denying its power" (2 Tim. 3:1-5). Yet the sure promise of God is that the time will come when the will of God shall be done on earth as in heaven. His children do not pray in vain: "Your will be done in earth, as it is in heaven."

Therefore, he would have his children — who have the earnest of the Spirit, the foretaste of future glory — pray day by day: "Hallowed be your name, your kingdom come, your will be done in earth, as it is in heaven." These prayers of the saints go up as incense before him, and when the victory is won, we shall know that God has won the victory in answer to those prayers. The seventy-second Psalm closes with the words, "The prayers of David, the son of Jesse, are ended." It is not literally true that the prayers of David were ended at that time, and careful interpreters believe that David meant that his prayers would be consummated when this Psalm was fulfilled: "Blessed be the Lord, the God of Israel, who alone does wondrous things. Blessed be his glorious name forever; may the whole earth be filled with his glory! Amen and Amen! The prayers of David, the son of Jesse, are ended." (Psa. 72:18-20).

In heaven the will of God is done perfectly by the angels. The result is perfect peace. Dr. Torrey used to give a glimpse of heaven and hell in such words as these: "Think of the moment of greatest darkness, of keenest anguish, of deepest sadness that human beings can suffer on earth. Multiply that by infinity, stretch it out to eternity, and we get a glimpse what hell is like. Think of the moment of greatest joy, of sweetest peace, of exhilaration of delight, you have known on earth. Multiply that by infinity, stretch out to eternity, and we get a glimpse of heaven."

In Bishop Edward Bickersteth's beautiful hymn "Peace, Perfect Peace" the question is asked, "Peace, perfect peace, by thronging duties pressed?" The answer is, "To do the will of Jesus, this is rest." A foretaste of eternal rest is to be in the will of God. Do we have that perfect peace? First of all, there must be the perfect peace that comes because we are justified by grace through faith in the shed blood of Christ. This is the will of God, that we should be born of the Spirit, and that we should be counted righteous before him. God intends that this perfect peace concerning our eternal safety in Christ should be linked with perfect peace concerning his present will for us.

It is possible to find the will of God, and to do it — although not perfectly as the Lord Jesus did because we are not yet sinless. But he is our Shepherd, supplying every need, and we shall not lack any good thing. If any Christian lacks wisdom, we may ask of God, who gives liberally, and upbraids not. The passion in the heart of every true believer is to do the will of God, in the big things and in the little things. The petition, "Your will be done," is a prayer for guidance. It is to be prayed in faith, without doubting, and the result will be: "the peace of God that surpasses all understanding shall guard your hearts and thought in Christ Jesus"(Phil. 4:7). As Isaiah 26:3 puts it, "You keep him in perfect peace whose mind is stayed on you, because he trusts in you." Thus do we enter today into a foretaste of that perfect peace of heaven. The one place of peace is in the center of the will of God.

Chapter 7

Give Us This Day Our Daily Bread

When we pray aright, we are seeking first the Kingdom of God and his righteousness (Matt. 6:33). When we obey that command, we may be very certain that God's promise will be fulfilled, "All these things will be added unto you." Our Lord in that Sermon on the Mount told the disciples not to be anxious about what they would eat, or drink, or wherewithal they would be clothed. We are to be anxious for nothing. We are to be absolutely confident that our heavenly Father will supply every material need. "Your heavenly Father knows that you need them all."

It is of God's free grace that all material needs are met. Yet he asks us to pray for these things. In the best known chapter of the Bible believers are told that the Lord is our Shepherd: we shall not want any good thing. The rest of the Psalm tells what these good things are. The Shepherd makes us to lie down in green pastures. He leads us beside the still waters. That is, we shall not lack the supply of any of our material needs. He restores our souls. We shall not lack forgiveness of sin. He guides us in the right path. We shall not lack guidance. He prepares a table before us in the presence of our enemies. We shall not lack victory over our enemies. Now notice that all of these things are ours, but in the Lord's Prayer we pray for these very things in the last four petitions.

The Lord is our Shepherd, making us to lie down in green pastures and leading us beside the still waters, but we pray: "Give us this day our daily bread."

The petition, "Give us this day our daily bread," reminds the Christian that everything we receive, we receive from the hand of the heavenly Father. Therefore all of our food and all of our material provisions should be received as directly from his hand, though we ourselves have a responsibility in providing these material things. "These all look to you, to give them their food in due season. When you give it to them, they gather it up; when you open your hand, they are filled with good things" (Psa. 104:27, 28). Do we sin by sitting down to a table provided by our heavenly Father without lifting our hearts in thanksgiving to him? Our Lord himself is our example in giving thanks. The Bible from beginning to end emphasizes this as the normal, natural thing, that a Christian should lift his heart in praise to God for his daily food. The islanders who were led to Christ by John G. Paton considered that one mark of the difference between the pagan who bows down to wood and stone and the Christian believer, is that the believers bow and give thanks at their meals. It would be a bit embarrassing to look into all the nominal Christian homes in America and discover whether there is a blessing at the meal time. But there would need to be the further question as to whether the blessing is merely a form of repetition of words rather than a genuine thanksgiving of the heart to the heavenly Father.

The petition, "Give us this day our daily bread," also teaches the Christian that he need never be anxious about the supply of every need.

On one occasion when the disciples got into the boat with the Lord they were concerned because they had forgotten to take any food with them. When the Lord said, "Watch out; beware of the leaven of the Pharisees and the leaven of Herod," and they began discussing with one another the fact that they had no bread (Mark 8:13-21). The Lord rebuked them for supposing that he was concerned about bread for the body. He asked them a striking question, "When I broke the five loaves for the five thousand, how many baskets full of broken pieces did you take up?" The answer was, "Twelve." This word "basket" refers to the small baskets that were carried by each of the disciples in their journeys. The Lord asked how many large baskets were taken up when the four thousand were fed. The answer was "seven." These baskets referred to hampers, like the one in which Paul was let down over the wall. Then the Lord asked them if they did not understand these miracles, and why they were concerned about bread. What a question it was. If the Lord Jesus, the mighty creator who was in their midst, could feed five thousand with five loaves and two fishes, and then see to it that just enough was left over to fill each one of their baskets; if the Lord could see that after the feeding of four thousand that there were seven large hampers left over, could the followers of such a Lord ever be concerned again with the supply of their material needs? Even the carnal, unbelieving multitude of the Jews caught the meaning of this miracle, when they wanted to come and by force make him king. A king who could do such marvels would never be defeated in battle. The prayer, "Give us this day our daily bread," can be prayed with absolute assurance that the need will be met.

It is related of C. H. Spurgeon that he was crossing the river Thames meditating on the verse, "Your grace is sufficient." Probably he needed the message just at that time, and he mused with himself: "Yes, I should say that God's grace is sufficient. It is as though a little bird should begin to worry about whether there was enough air for him to breathe and sufficient atmosphere for his flying. The air replies, 'don't worry, little bird, I have enough air for you.' Or as though a little fish in the Thames should begin to wonder whether he will always have enough supply of water, and Father Thames says, 'Don't worry, little fish, I have sufficient water to take care of all your needs."

The oft-quoted lines of Elizabeth Cheney's poem "Overheard in an Orchard" illustrate the truth of God's sufficiency, and bring conviction to our worrying hearts:

> Said the Robin to the Sparrow,
> "I should really like to know
> Why these anxious human beings,
> Rush about and worry so."

> Said the Sparrow to the Robin,
> "Friend, I think that it must be
> That they have no Heavenly Father
> Such as cares for you and me."

The word that our English translators render "daily," is a Greek word that occurs only in the two passages giving our Lord's Prayer, and nowhere else in Greek literature in or out of the Bible. There is a difference of opinion as to whether the word is based on the verb "to be," or on a word that means "to come." Thus there are two possible literal translations, "our bread for the coming day," and "our essential bread." Does it seem likely that the Lord would ask us to pray today for our bread for the coming day, except in the sense that we should not be anxious for the morrow? The expression "our daily bread," does suggest our necessary material needs for this day, and it would seem that the true meaning of the word is "our essential bread." We have been speaking particularly of our material needs, and this is doubtless the primary meaning in the Lord's Prayer. However, it is natural when we think of the supply of our daily bread to remember that bread is ever a symbol of Christ who is the living bread. Even as we pray for material things, and thank him for the supply, we take these things as a token that we have Christ who is the true bread, that is, the real bread that comes down from heaven.

Now there are Christians who from the beginning of their lives until they go to be with the Lord never have occasion to wonder where their material supply is coming from. There are other Christians who need to look to the Lord day by day for material needs. The more normal thing is that Christians do have a more or less assured income. But for the Christian the income is not assured merely because he has lifetime job with a good company. It is assured because the Lord is supplying the needs. They can recognize it as coming from the Lord, even though they are not tested in this matter as some are who are called to live by faith. George Mueller was used by the Lord to teach millions of Christians the lesson of faith by his trust that the heavenly Father would supply the material needs for his family of orphan children that grew to number many thousands. On a grand scale, this work and similar works are illustrations of the answer of this petition, "Give us this day our daily bread."

Sophie the scrubwoman has given us a lesson on the meaning of this petition for our daily bread. Thousands all over the world are indebted to the Rev. H. B. Gibbud for passing on two of Sophie's "Sermons." A unique figure for years in Christian circles in New York City, Sophie, who was called to scrub and preach was always witnessing for Christ and used practically all her earnings for missionary work. The following is an extract from Sophie's Sermon, as told by Mr. Gibbud:

"'How do you live, and yet have so much to give away?' I asked.

"'Oh, I live plain; my clothes cost me nothing much. I haf a cup of coffee und roll for my breakfast, and get my other meals where I work.

I only haf one small room; that is all I want here, but, praise God, I haf a mansion in Heaven. My Elder Brutter he vas making it ready for me, und he is coming again to take me there, He promised; und if I die before he come, that will only be moving from the tenement into the mansion; und there will be no rent to pay, und no mortgage on it either. What I needs here Father sends. I can trust him. Is not two sparrows sold for a farthing? That bird he nefer goes to church; und yet the Book says he nefer falls to the ground without Father knows it; und I vas worth more, cause I vas his child. We forgets how he minds us; but he never forgets us. Only the other day I vas learned a lesson on that thing.

"'In the mornink I always get down the Bible. I call it my love-letter from Father. Sometimes he scolds a little in the letter; but it vas for "reproof and correction;" und we need that sometimes. Well this mornink I open to the prayer, "Our Father which vas in Heaven," und I says, "Oh, Father! I know that by heart; gif me something fresh." So I read something else. That mornink I haf no money to get the coffee and roll; but I did not worry. I thought I gets my breakfast where I vas to work; but they vas all through when I got there. "Well," I say, "nefer mind, I wait till dinner." Before dinner the woman goes out und forgets all about me; so no dinner. I got through early, und I vas so hungry I go home ready to cry, und I say, "Father, how is this; You say You nefer leave me; but I work all day without anything to eat " Und I began to complain. "Look here, Sophie", said Father, almost speaking to my soul plain. "Look here; this mornink you read in My Book, und when you comes to the prayer where it says, 'Gif me this day my daily bread,' you don't read it; you say, 'Gif me something fresh.' Is that stale? Because every day these things come you forget to be thankful." At once I see where I sin, und gets down und say, "Father, forgive me, gif me this day my daily bread, for Thy child is hungry.

"'When I got off my knees there came a knock, und my landlady vas there with a cup of coffee und some biscuits. She said, "I thought you were tired, und might not like to get supper; so I brought these in.' Then I thank Father, und begin to shout.

"'I tell you, brutter, we so quick forgetting those everyday blessings what comes right along. So many peoples nefer are polite enough to say, Thank you, God for the hundreds of everday gifts. The landlady's husband heard me shouting, and came up. He is an infidel; but he vas touched when I told him the answer my prayer.

"'The woman was a Catholic, und she says, "Sophie, you always praise Jesus, und talk about Jesus. Why you nefer talk about the blessed Virgin? I pray to her, und expect to see her in Heaven." Well, I told her if she ever expected to see the mother of Jesus she must first get acquainted with the Son, or she would nefer get into Heaven.

"Well," she said, "don't Peter hold the keys?" I told her I did not care who held the keys; that Jesus said, "I am the Door; by Me if any man enter in, he shall be saved." Und as I had the open door, I did not care who had the keys.

"'It is precious to have Jesus only, and to live for him. But now I must go, brutter. I will come again if my Father will let me.'

"I saw her to the door, bade her goodbye, returned to my room, and thanked God for the sermon to which I had listened. I had been sitting in heavenly places in an atmosphere of heaven that seemed to lift me into Jesus Christ. There was about the plain scrub-woman a closer relationship to God, my Father. The lessons I learned of trust and fellowship with Christ, from her talk, have been helps toward the Golden City and the King; and I look forward with pleasure to the time when I shall have another opportunity to listen to one of Sophie's sermons."

Chapter 8

Forgive Us Our Debts

The petition, "Give us this day our daily bread," is a constant reminder that we are finite creatures, dependent on our creator for the supply of every material need. If God withdraws his bread, we return to dust. We are continually upheld by the hand of him who created us.

The next petition, "Forgive us our debts," reminds us constantly that we are not only creatures created by God, but we are sinners. If we have taken Christ as our Saviour, we are children of God and we may come boldly into his presence. Nevertheless, we are not yet sinless. We come into his presence only because of the merit of the blood of Christ. He has opened the new and living way. He is our great Priest, interceding before God.

When we come to pray, our one ground of entrance into God's holy presence is the blood of Christ and the righteousness of Christ. There is no moment in our lives when we do not need the blood of Christ, no moment in our lives when we do not need the intercession of our great High Priest. This means that we are not sinless while we are in the body. We need to confess our sins.

Some of the old English translations render this petition: "Forgive us our trespasses, as we forgive those who trespass against us." This translation passed into the prayer book used by the English church, and is the form used in many of the churches. The word means the same, whether we speak of debts, or trespasses, or sins.

This petition in the Lord's Prayer has been the occasion of much theological discussion, but there are millions of humble-hearted Christians who have never had any difficulty in using this petition and knowing just what it means.

There are those who teach that a Christian should be entirely sanctified in this life, and that while in this state of sanctification he does not sin. The question would arise as to whether he can pray this prayer. Our Lord himself could never pray this petition. He did not give the prayer as one that he himself would use, although as the Son of man he could use every petition of this prayer except, "Forgive us our debts." He was sinless, and never had any sins to confess. Does any Christian get to the place where he can omit this petition? No serious student of the Bible would claim that he does. Those who teach that Christians do not sin, nevertheless tell us that Christians have infirmities which need the blood of Christ for cleansing, and which need this petition, "Forgive us our debts." If that is so, these infirmities are of the nature of sin.

Those who teach that Christians may become sinless are using a different definition for "sin." The sainted John Wesley himself readily agreed that if sin means any want of conformity unto or transgression of the perfect moral law of God, then no man in the flesh ever reaches that standard. But he spoke of a lower standard, a standard of "Christian perfection," or "evangelical obedience." Yet Wesley recognized not only that no man had infallible assurance that he was in this state of perfection, but also that those who were "entirely sanctified" needed the blood of Christ for their infirmities, and needed to pray this prayer.

However, there has been a more serious challenge to this petition because of the words that follow the prayer for forgiveness: "Forgive us our debts, as we forgive our debtors."

There are Christian teachers who tell us that the Lord's Prayer is on legal ground and should not be prayed by Christians under grace. In Ephesians 4:32 we read: "Be kind to one another, tenderhearted, forgiving one another, as God in Christ forgave you." This is said to be the plan of God under grace. We have already been forgiven. Because of this, we are exhorted to forgive one another. But in the Lord's Prayer the matter is reversed, they say; we ask God to forgive our debts on the ground that we have forgiven others. This is said to be under law, rather than under grace. It is intended for the Jews before Pentecost, and in the coming Kingdom age.

The plain meaning of this teaching is that these believers who pray the Lord's Prayer have their sins forgiven because of something that they themselves have done. There is merit in their forgiving others, and in recognition of that merit, their sins are forgiven. This would mean that God has two plans of salvation, one by grace through faith, for believers in the present age, and another plan of salvation by works, at least partly by works. But if there is one slightest particle of works, or human merit, then grace is destroyed. All Christians know, when they clearly study the matter, that salvation is by grace through faith, and has been by grace through faith for every sinner from the time of Adam on. All people who were saved in the Old Testament period were saved by grace through faith.

But this petition in the Lord's Prayer does not raise a difficulty like that. Let us recall how the Lord's Prayer opens: "Our Father in heaven." This prayer is to be prayed only by children of God, who have been born of the Spirit through faith in Christ. It is a family matter. Those who pray "forgive us our debts," have already been cleansed through the blood of Christ. God, for the Saviour's sake, has already forgiven our sins. Since that is so, the love of God shed abroad in our hearts by the Holy Spirit leads us to have a forgiving spirit toward others. The Westminster Catechism expresses this clearly: "In the fifth petition, which is, and forgive us our debts as we forgive our debtors, we pray that God, for Christ's sake, will freely pardon all of our sins; which we are the rather encouraged to ask because by his grace we are enabled from the heart to forgive others." Thus the forgiving of others is not the ground for God's forgiveness, nor the measure of it, but the evidence that we have humble hearts that are ready to confess sins and be forgiven.

Several years ago, at the close of a young people's conference, a deeply spiritual Bible teacher came to the writer for an interview, saying she had recently heard the teaching that the Lord's prayer was not designed for Christians, because it conditioned forgiveness of our sins upon our forgiving others. We discussed the meaning of this petition and the fact that only children of God could pray the Lord's Prayer.

While this conversation was going on, a young woman with a troubled, rather sullen face, was waiting. "Can I talk with you?" she said. "You know the girl who said in her testimony tonight that there was a girl she had not been speaking to for six weeks. Well, I am that girl that she was talking about."

"Have you decided now to go and make up with her?"

"I don't see why I can't have victory in my life. I have surrendered everything else except that."

"Let us sit here, and talk about it. But first let us pray. You pray."

After a moment of silence, I said, "Pray the Lord's prayer."

I had never made that kind of suggestion to anyone before. But the young woman obediently began to pray, like a child, in a petulant way: "Our Father, who art in heaven. Hallowed be thy name. Thy kingdom come, Thy will be done, on earth as it is in heaven. Give us this day our daily bread . . ."

"What's the matter?" No answer. "Why don't you go on?" Still no answer. "How have you been praying for the last six weeks?"

"Haven't prayed."

And thus did the Holy Spirit convict by this word of the living God. This young girl had not prayed for six weeks. No one can pray who deliberately refuses to forgive another. He can only "say prayers." And none can be assured of answers to prayer who holds an unforgiving spirit. This young woman did surrender her life, and ask forgiveness of her sin; needless to say the first thing she planned to do was to go to her friend and ask forgiveness, having first forgiven her from her heart.

It is true that our Lord gave further revelation concerning prayer, and it is true that when Christ died and rose again there was a new meaning to praying in his name. But this did not abrogate the teaching he had given before. The marvelous thing about the revelation of Christ is that he gives eternal truth that fits in perfectly with further revelations that are given. All that is said in the Lord's Prayer is in the name of Christ, although the words are not used.

Another reason given for considering the prayer not for Christians is that praise and thanksgiving are not included. But "Hallowed be Your name," rings with praise and glory and thanksgiving. Even if the prayer did belong only to the Old Testament it should ring with praise and it should ring with grace, for at the very heart of the Old Testament revelation is the grace of God, and its very breath is thanksgiving and praise.

Distress and division have come in churches where it has been taught that it is wrong for Christians to use the Lord's Prayer. There is no question that the prayer is often used in a mechanical way, and harmfully used by great crowds of people. But this does not alter the fact that the words are full of marvelous meaning, and have depths of instruction concerning true prayer for every Christian who will be taught of the Spirit, and will take these words as a guide for his own prayer.

Now the question arises, suppose we do not forgive others? Will we then be forgiven? It is a striking fact that on no other petition does the Lord himself make any comment, but after giving the Lord's Prayer in the Sermon on the Mount he adds: "For if you forgive others their trespasses, your heavenly Father will also forgive you, but if you do not forgive others their trespasses, neither will your Father forgive your trespasses" (Matt. 6:14, 15). We remember in this connection the solemn teaching of the parable of the unmerciful servant, who having been forgiven a debt of ten million dollars (worth ten or twenty times that much today), refused to have mercy on a fellow servant who owed him seventeen dollars. The lord of this unmerciful servant was angry, "and put him in prison until he should pay the debt." There follows our Lord's solemn comment: "So also my heavenly Father will do to every one of you, if you do not forgive your brother from your heart" (Matt. 18:35).

Again, when our Lord gave the challenge to prayer in Mark 11:22-25, "Have faith in God", he added the words, "And whenever you stand praying, forgive, if you have anything against anyone, so that your Father also who is in heaven may forgive you your trespasses" (Mark 22:25).

Our Lord knew the human heart, and he knew that one of the greatest hindrances to getting our prayers answered is a lack of forgiving love toward others; we would be right with God, we must be right with men.

The question rises as to whether these solemn warnings are

pronounced against professing Christians who are not really saved, or against real Christians. Are we in danger of making forgiveness a matter of works, and securing forgiveness from God because of our own merit in forgiving others? It is not a solution of this problem to say that the Lord intended these warnings for Jews and not for us. If that is so, there is on one hand the difficulty that God is forgiving sins and saving people for some other reason than on the ground of Christ's blood and righteousness. On the other hand, there is the complete ignoring of the warning that we Christians need regarding the importance of forgiving others.

The fact is, as someone has put it, "An unforgiving heart is an unforgiven heart." A professing Christian who will not forgive others may be in one of two classes. He may be simply a professing Christian who has never known the grace of God in his heart. He gives evidence of the fact that his own sins have never been forgiven, by his hardness of heart in refusing to forgive others. On the other hand, there are Christians who have really been saved and yet fall into the sin of not forgiving others. These Christians will be chastened by the Lord. Paul told the Corinthians that the reason some of them were sick and others had died was because of their spiritual condition (1 Cor. 11:30-32). When a Christian prays the Lord's prayer, "Forgive us our debts, as we forgive our debtors," he is not praying that he may accept Christ as his Saviour. He already has done this. His sins are under the blood. Nevertheless he needs to confess and forsake his sin. He does not have the root sin of rejecting Christ. If lack of forgiveness of others indicates he has that root sin of rejecting Christ, this means that he never has been a child of God. On the other hand, if he is a child of God and does not forgive others, then he continues in a state of broken fellowship with Christ. His own spiritual life is hindered, and he will be chastened of the Lord even to the extent of being put to death in the flesh that the spirit may he saved (1 Cor. 5:5).

But after all, these petitions are for Christians who are abiding in the Lord, and who want him to have his way, Christians who do, by God's grace, forgive others. The petition "Forgive us our debts," does not mean that we should make this petition cover all of our confession of sin. There are those who say, indeed, that we ought not to pray for forgiveness. Christians, they say, are to confess their sins according to the command in 1 John 1:9: "If we confess our sins, he is faithful and just to forgive us our sins, and to cleanse us from all unrighteousness." But this is a mere play on words. This petition means that very thing; in this way we do confess our sins.

There are the definite sins of which the Holy Spirit convicts us. We are to confess these to the Lord. We are also to confess them to anyone whom we have injured. There is grave danger in going to extremes and in confessing secret sins in public, or to those who are not concerned. Some Christians have caused harm and have lost friends by confessing some secret thought they had in their minds concerning another. When the Holy Spirit is in control, He will guide about what confessions should be made. However, the principle is that our confessions should be made to those against whom we have sinned, or those who know that we have committed a particular sin.

One reason it is easier for us to confess to the Lord than to people is because our confession to the Lord often is not really confession. When the Holy Spirit convicts us of the horror of sin, he convicts the Christian of sinning against the love of Christ. This conviction is so real and deep that it seems to matter not what human beings may know about it. Nevertheless, the confession to men does bring us face to face with the seriousness of the sins we have committed.

Again, the Christian may not have been guilty of any sin of commission, that he is conscious of, yet he needs to pray, "Forgive us our debts." The nearer one gets to Christ, the more conscious he is of the heinousness of sin, and of the sinfulness of his own heart, apart from God's grace. The approach of the Lord's prayer to the Father is the approach of all prayer, through the new and living way opened into the most Holy Place by the blood of our Great High Priest (Heb. 10:19-22).

Chapter 9

Lead Us Not Into Temptation

Many Protestant scholars consider that the Lord's Prayer contains six petitions. Thus the Shorter Catechism of the Westminster Assembly answers the question, "What do we pray for in the sixth petition?" as follows: "In the sixth petition, which is, 'And lead us not into temptation, but deliver us from evil,' we pray that God would either keep us from being tempted to sin, or support and deliver us when we are tempted."

Other scholars consider the words, "deliver us from evil," as a seventh petition. There is certainly a close connection between the prayer to lead us not into temptation, and the prayer to deliver from evil. But there are advantages in considering them separately.

What is meant by the petition, "Lead us not into temptation?" In what sense can God lead us into temptation? We are told, "Let no one say when he is tempted, "I am being tempted by God," for God cannot be tempted with evil, and he himself tempts no one" (James 1:13).

The word "temptation" is used in two distinct senses in Scripture. It is used in the sense of testing, or trial, as in James 1:2, "Count it all joy, my brothers, when you meet trials of various kinds." It is used in the sense of a solicitation to evil. It is primarily in this sense that the word is used in the Lord's Prayer, although we need to recognize that testings or trials may be the occasion of a temptation to unbelief or to other sin.

The form of the petition, "Lead us not into temptation," does not suggest that it is God who leads into a temptation that may result in sin. The positive way of putting this temptation would be: "Lead me, O Lord, in your righteousness" (Psa. 5:8), or "Lead me in your truth, and teach me" (Psa. 25:5), or "Lead me on a level path" (Psa. 27:11). So in the twenty-third Psalm we read: "He leads me in the paths of righteousness for his name's sake." The Lord "leads us not" into temptation in the sense that he leads and guides us into right paths.

Note also that in this expression, "Lead us not into temptation," we have an example of a common Hebrew idiom. In praying to God, we recognize that God has complete control over all things. To him, therefore, may be ascribed everything. God is never the author of evil, but he does permit evil for his own wise purposes. Therefore, the Scripture writers ascribe directly to God the things that he permits, and prayer may be made to God that he shall not permit these things. Thus the Psalmist prays, "Do not drag me off with the wicked, with the workers of evil" (Psa. 28:3). Again, "Do not sweep my soul away with sinners, nor my life with bloodthirsty men" (Psa. 26:9). The Psalmist might have prayed, "Prevent Satan from doing this." So our petition might read, "Do not permit us to be tempted so as to sin."

In every petition we are faced with the mystery of prayer, and its place in the providence of God. One might say that God will keep his children, and will not lead them into temptation that might result in sin, even though they do not pray this prayer. But we have our Lord's command, "Watch and pray that you may not enter into temptation. The spirit indeed is willing, but the flesh is weak" (Matt. 26:41). What a teaching on prayer is this! Consider the teacher and the occasion. It is in the midst of his own agonizing prayer in the garden. He is watching and praying, and when he comes and finds the disciples asleep, he says to Peter: "what, could you not watch with me one hour?" Peter, in his confidence that he would never betray his Lord, did not watch and pray against that temptation. When we pray, "Lead us not into temptation," we are carrying out the Lord's command, "Watch and pray that you may not enter into temptation."

Watching and praying describes the constant attitude of the Christian. He is in a warfare. He is to be on guard, just as the soldier and the general in a critical battle. Watchfulness is never to be relaxed. The most shameful lesson in all American history of the lack of watchfulness was in the disaster at Pearl Harbor on December 7, 1941. Abundant warning had been given that there was a strong and subtle and treacherous enemy. Yet the enemy came in an hour that they thought not, and found the greatest nation on earth utterly unprepared.

So a Christian, or a Christian church, or a Christian community, often goes down into defeat by a sudden onslaught of the enemy for which we are unprepared. But we are to watch always. This does not mean to be at high tension, or to have a disturbed mind, but to recognize that Satan is going about as a roaring lion seeking whom he may devour. Greater is he that is in us than he that is in the world, and Christ has won the victory over Satan. Nevertheless, his plan is that we should enter into this victory through prayer.

We have this sure promise: "No temptation has overtaken you that is not common to man. God is faithful, and he will not let you be tempted beyond your ability, but with the temptation he will also provide the way of escape, that you may be able to endure it" (1 Cor. 10:13). Here we may consider the word "temptation" as including trials and testings, and also the solicitation to sin. Let us consider God's way of dealing with both kinds of temptation.

In dealing with trials and tribulations and testings, God's way is precisely the opposite of the natural human way. We might expect this.

His ways are not as our ways. He tells us to count it all joy when we fall into various kinds of trials (James 1:2). We count it all joy when we fall out of these testings. He tells us to glory in tribulations. Sophie the scrubwoman in one of her "sermons" reminds us that glory is not spelled g-r-o-w-l. Yet it is the natural thing to growl about our trials and tribulations.

God's Word always deals with reality. There is among the modern religions a teaching that professes to be the secret of joy and peace and deliverance: "Don't worry. There's nothing to worry about. Sin is not real. Sickness is not real. Tribulation is not real. The way to deal with them is to recognize that these things do not actually exist." These are cruel lies. Sin is real. Sickness and trials are very real. The Lord is not saying to us, "Cheer up: there is nothing to worry about." On the contrary, he says, "In the world you will have tribulation. But take heart; I have overcome the world" (John 16:33).

The secret is that just as God in his marvelous grace has turned the cross, the emblem of deepest shame, into the greatest glory, so he is able to use trials and tribulations for blessing. We are to count it all joy when we fall into trials, "for you know that the testing of your faith produces steadfastness. And let steadfastness have its full effect, that you may be perfect and complete, lacking in nothing." (James 1:3, 4). The same teaching is given through Paul: "Not only that, but we rejoice in our sufferings, knowing that suffering produces endurance, and endurance produces character, and character produces hope, and hope does not put us to shame, because God's love has been poured into our hearts through the Holy Spirit who has been given to us" (Rom. 5:3-5).

There is a reason given why we should glory in tribulation; not because of the trials themselves, but because of what God by his grace works for us through the trials. The words used are picture words:

"tribulation" is the thing that presses down; "steadfastness" is that which holds up under. It is like the old method of testing the strength of concrete floors; enormous weights were piled on the floors to test them; when the floors were strong they held up under, and passed the test. So steadfastness works out approvedness, or the passing of the test. Approvedness works out "hope," that is, hope of the glory of God, hope of being conformed to the image of Christ. This is not a hope that puts to shame, as though we had nothing to show for it.

The writer some years ago met an earnest, optimistic Christian who possessed property on which he believed there was a valuable gold mine. He consulted with me as to investing many thousands of dollars in missionary work. Had I set my hope upon this, it would have been a hope that put to shame. The gold mine never materialized. But our hope of being like Christ is not a hope that puts to shame, because the love of God has been shed abroad in our hearts by the Holy Spirit who has been given unto us. The Holy Spirit is an earnest of our inheritance, the firstfruits of the full harvest. The assurance of future conformity to the image of Christ, is present likeness to Christ, produced by the working of the Holy Spirit.

This, then, is God's glorious use of trials and tribulations and testings. Testing is God's molding chisel to mold us into the image of Christ. Therefore, we can say: "And we know that for those who love God all things work together for good, for those who are called according to his purpose" (Rom. 8:28). As someone has remarked of this promise, it is not that all things work together for "goods," but for the real "good." What is that? It is the purpose of God. It is conformity to the image of his Son (Romans 8:29).

At a conference some years ago a group of us were visiting together at the close of a meeting. In the group was a devoted minister who seemed to be overflowing with joy. Someone remarked that he seemed to be quite happy. He said that it was the happiest week of his life. Then he gave this testimony:

"In recent weeks I have been meeting so many trials and difficulties that I have been almost in despair. Things piled up more and more. Finally, it seemed that I could bear it no longer, and I threw myself before the Lord with the cry in my heart: 'O Lord, when am I going to get out of all these troubles?' I suppose my mind was so pressed that I did not know exactly what words I was using, and I found myself saying: 'O Lord, what am I going to get out of all these troubles?'

"When I prayed that prayer, the Spirit seemed to flash across my mind immediately the message that God uses trials to bring blessing and glory. I began to meditate on what God purposed that his children should get out of trials, and my heart was filled with joy.

"Now," he added facetiously, "the only trouble is that the trials are disappearing so rapidly that I am afraid that I may miss some of the blessings."

We need not pray for testings to come. The humble attitude is to pray that they may not come if they would be the occasion of failure. We can pray that only such trials and testing may come as God can work out for his own glory. We know that God does permit testings to come to his children, and we also know that he himself may bring these testings, as he tested Abraham. But he never tempts us to evil.

In order that our prayer against temptation to sin may be intelligent, we should know the way temptation comes, and how to meet it. Dr. Melvin Grove Kyle gave this definition: "Temptation is the incitement of a natural desire to go beyond the bound set by God." We might word it this way: "Temptation is an appeal to a natural desire to be used contrary to the will of God."

James, in warning us that God does not tempt any man, explains how temptation comes: "But each person is tempted when he is lured and enticed by his own desire. Then desire when it has conceived gives birth to sin, and sin when it is fully grown brings forth death" (James 1:14, 15). We have used the translation "desire," as being more accurate than the word "lust." The word lust means sinful desire. But these natural desires are not in themselves sinful, although they are the desires of men with fallen, sinful human natures.

What are those desires? The Bible consistently presents all the desires that a human being may have as included in three. Dr. Kyle summed up these three desires in his concise way: "We have the desire to enjoy things, the desire to get things, the desire to do things." The desire to enjoy things concerns all the appetites of our bodies, what we may enjoy through our senses. The desire to get things concerns all the world that is outside ourselves, the things we can get possession of. The desire to accomplish things concerns all that we may do to affect that world outside ourselves.

It will be seen at once that temptation came to Adam and Eve through these three desires. Eve saw that the tree was good for food. That is, the fruit made an appeal to her desire to enjoy good things with her body. There was nothing sinful in this desire. God gave that desire. God filled the Garden of Eden with all good things to satisfy that desire. The temptation was an appeal to that desire to satisfy it in a way contrary to God's will. She saw that the fruit was a delight to the eyes. This was an appeal to her desire to get possession of things. It was a perfectly right desire. God made man with the purpose of giving him dominion over the earth. All things belonged to man, except the one thing that God had forbidden. The third desire implanted in man was the desire to be like God. This was God's purpose for man. The temptation from the enemy was to eat the forbidden fruit, with the promise that her eyes would be opened, and that she would become like God. This temptation was an appeal to a right desire to be like God, but to use the desire in disobedience to God's will.

It is to be noted that this temptation came to human beings who were sinless. Because they were human beings, they had these three desires, which belong to human nature, apart from sin.

Likewise when our Lord, the second Man from heaven, the last Adam, was tempted, he was tempted in these three ways. When we read that our Lord was tempted in all points like as we are, we must never suppose that our Lord had all the individual temptations that come to sinful man. He was tempted on all sides of his human nature. Our Lord Jesus had these three desires. He had the natural desire to enjoy food for his body. He was hungry, and the desire to eat food was a perfectly right desire. Adam and Eve were tempted in the midst of the luxury and abundance of the Garden of Eden. Sin turned that garden into a wilderness. Our Lord was tempted in the wilderness, after he had fasted for forty days and forty nights. The Tempter came and asked him to satisfy that hunger in a wrong way.

There has been a discussion as to whether Christ could sin. On the one hand, if we suppose it possible for the Lord Jesus to have given way before the Tempter, then we may say that God's whole plan of redemption was hanging on a possibility. On the other hand, it is contended that if it was not possible for Christ to sin, it was not possible for him to be tempted. But this is to mistake the nature of temptation. The temptation was just as real as the hunger. The temptation was an incitement of his desire to satisfy his hunger. The Tempter suggested that this hunger should be satisfied in a wrong way. Temptation is not sin, and in the case of our Lord there was no slightest taint of sin in his meeting of the temptation. When we are facing the mystery of the divine and human natures in Christ we cannot always explain the facts fully. Christ was not tempted in his divine nature, but in his human nature. God cannot be tempted. Nevertheless, the Lord Jesus is one person. He is God as well as man. Sin is against God, and in this sense we say it is impossible to conceive of Christ's sinning. He was indeed touched with a feeling of our infirmity, because he was tempted on all sides of his human nature, yet apart from sin.

The temptation to secure all the kingdoms of the earth in a moment of time was an appeal to a perfectly right desire. Christ came to win back from Satan all the kingdoms of the earth. Man through his sin lost dominion over those kingdoms. It is God's purpose to restore those kingdoms to man. Christ is heir of the world, the head of redeemed humanity. But that conquest was to come through the cross, God's way, and not Satan's way. The third temptation was an appeal to Christ's desire to be accepted as Israel's Messiah. If he should cast himself down from the temple, and multitudes should see angels bear him up in their hands, then they would accept this sign and receive the Messiah, so the Tempter suggested. The longing desire in the heart of Christ was that his people might receive him as Messiah. The temptation was an appeal to this right desire, a suggestion to satisfy the desire contrary to the will of God.

Since there are these three temptations, or these three avenues of temptation, there are also three sins which comprehend all other sins. When the desire to enjoy things leads to the use of the bodily appetites in a way contrary to the will of God, we call it the lust of the flesh. When the desire to get possession of things, or to use money, is satisfied in a way that is contrary to God's will, we call it the lust of the eye, or covetousness. When the highest of human desires, what we call ambition, the desire to accomplish something, to make the most of our abilities, leads to a life that does not put God in the center, we call it the sin of pride, or the vainglory of life, going after the things that man glories in rather than the glory of the only God. Thus, the Spirit sums up these three sins in the remarkable passage in 1 John 2:15-17, "Do not love the world or the things in the world. If anyone loves the world, the love of the Father is not in him. For all that is in the world — the desires of the flesh and the desires of the eyes and pride of life — is not from the Father but is from the world. And the world is passing away along with its desires, but whoever does the will of God abides forever."

We have noticed that these three desires are desires that belong to human nature. They were the desires of Adam and Eve before sin entered. They were the desires of the sinless Son of man. But what of these desires in sinful man? Does temptation come in the same way? Temptation does not strike what we might call sinful things in a man. They already are on Satan's side. Temptation is an appeal to the natural desires to use them in a sinful way. We still have the desires. However, since sin has entered into the human race, we are fallen human beings. This is expressed popularly by saying that every man, including every Christian, has a sinful nature. But this expression "sinful nature" does not mean some entity injected into man, as though this thing were separate from the man himself. Our human nature is a fallen, sinful human nature, and therefore all our desires are affected by this fact. It is not a sin to eat to satisfy hunger. It is not a sin for a man and woman to have affection for one another and to be married. It is not a sin to make money and to use money. It is not a sin to have ambition. But the expression of our fallen human nature is to put self in the center and not to do all things for the glory of God. Our Lord met these temptations by recognizing God's principle that man shall not live by bread alone, that man should not worship Satan (that is, he should not have the covetousness which is idolatry, but should use all material things alone for God's glory), that man should not seek the glory that is of man, the vainglory of life, but do all things with the ambition of being like Christ and glorifying God.

But what bearing has all this on the petition: "Lead us not into temptation"? When we are aware of the channels of temptation, we are certain of two things. The first is that Satan is too strong an enemy for us, and that our own sinful human nature will naturally lead us into sin. Set over against this is the glorious fact of the Gospel that Christ has defeated Satan, that we have the Holy Spirit living in our hearts, giving spiritual life to our sin-cursed bodies, which are not yet completely redeemed. Recognizing our weakness and his power, we pray in humility: "Lead us not into temptation." When we pray that prayer we must do it in the spirit of hating everything in the least tainted with these three sins of lust, covetousness, and pride.

The most sacred of all human relations is the marriage relationship. There is an expression of affection that belongs to this marriage relationship which belongs to one man and one woman, bound together in the holy bonds of matrimony. The temptation to the sin of the lust of the flesh is the stirring up of natural human desires connected with our affections to be used contrary to the will of God. All would recognize that adultery is sin. Men use the same physical powers in committing an act of adultery that are used in the pure and right marital relations (Heb. 13:4). There is no question that the United States of America in our generation is facing the greatest breakdown in moral standards that the nation has ever known. When we pray, "Lead us not into temptation," we should recognize that the sin of the lust of the flesh begins when we give way to any desire in thought, word or deed that is contrary to the high standards of God's purity. When a young woman permits any young man to take liberty with her by expressing his affection in kissing or caressing her (unless she is bound by the solemn covenant of engagement to be married to the young man, in the will of God), then that young woman is sinning the lust of the flesh, and she is offering her body as an instrument for sin in the young man. All would admit that a wife or a husband should not express affection by kissing or caressing any other man or woman. They are bound together in the sacred bonds of matrimony, and thus she is separated from all other men and he from all other women in that relationship. The same principle applies to all men and women who are not married.

Our Lord in interpreting the inner meaning of the Old Testament command, "You shall not commit adultery," declared, "Everyone who looks at a woman with lustful intent has already committed adultery with her in his heart" (Matt. 5:28). Our Lord, of course, did not mean that it was as bad to have the inward desire as to commit the outward act. In the case of the outward act, the desire has come to its culmination. But he was warning us against the very beginning of the sin of lust. He is revealing that sin begins in the inmost desire, whether that desire be expressed in word or act.

There is no question in the mind of any serious student of morals, whether he be a Christian believer or not, that a great influence in breaking down all the defenses that men have had against chastity and immorality is the moving picture industry in America. Many thoughtful leaders would say that it is the greatest demoralizing influence of an outward sort that has ever come to our nation. Yet with these facts so plain that all can read them, we have an almost universal acceptance of the practice of movie-going, on the part of churches and church leaders. Millions of Christians pray, "Lead us not into temptation," and then they organize their lives in such a way that their children are trained from their earliest years to give way to the temptations of the lust of the flesh. Thus a noted writer on the subject can refer to "Our Movie-Made Children," with the assurance that all will understand that this is the truth.

When we pray, "Lead us not into temptation" we should shun evil. We should fear the very beginning of any temptation that is connected with lack of purity. This breakdown of standards encouraged by movies and by the life of the actors and actresses is reflected in our novels and magazines. The vile suggestiveness of the written word, and of the pictures, does not mean that these sins are new sins. It does mean that in our modern life we are making attractive the sins that destroy the human soul. God's law was intended to reveal the exceeding sinfulness of sin. America indeed needs a conviction of sin, a facing of the terrors of the law of God.

The second great sin is the sin of covetousness. Here again, men condemn the final outworking of covetousness. At the time of this writing in 1943, we have no difficulty in seeing the horror of the sin of Germany and Japan when they covet other nations and go to every length to conquer them.

But where is the suggestion of any conviction of sin on the part of the United States of America, which furnished Japan with about sixty percent of all the weapons with which she conducted the cruelest war in all the history of civilized nations? Many excuses may be given, but behind this act of America was simple, unadulterated covetousness. God's laws apply not to individual Christians only, but to all men and to all nations. "Sexually immoral people and adulterers God will judge."

So also covetous men and nations God will judge. Already we are seeing that every dollar we gain by trade with Japan will be paid for a thousand-fold, not in money only but in precious lives. This is not to say that precious lives would not need to be given had we not sinned the sin of covetousness. But it is to say that God sometimes uses war to punish nations for their national sins.

When we pray, "Lead us not into temptation," we are asking that God might allow us to use every dollar that comes into our possession for the glory of God. The teaching of the Bible with regard to money is that men are stewards. They are responsible for the individual owner-ship of property so far as other men are concerned. But God owns all property. Not a dollar and not a foot of ground is our own. The Lord in one of the parables referred to the rich fool. We speak of the "poor fool." The rich man was a fool because he thought the money was his own. So is every rich man who uses the money as though it belonged to him rather than belonging to God.

When we pray, "Lead us not into temptation," we are praying that the Lord's command may be fulfilled: "Take care, and be on your guard against all covetousness, for one's life does not consist in the abundance of his possessions"(Luke 12:15). We are praying that we might follow God's will in the giving of our money to carry out Christ's passion that the Gospel should be preached in the uttermost part of the earth. We are praying that we might seek first the Kingdom of God and his righteousness, that we might be rich toward God, and lay up treasures in heaven. For the temptation to covetousness is a temptation to turn away from the consideration of the unseen world and the true riches.

Finally, "Lead us not into temptation" is the prayer that whatever we do, whether we eat or drink or whatsoever we do, we should do all to the glory of God in the name of the Lord Jesus (Col. 3:17). The difference between the children of this age and the children of light is precisely this, that the one seeks the glory that is of man, and the other seeks the glory that is of God. The most ominous fact in the midst of the world conflict in which our nation is engaged is the fact that man's glory is ever set before us, and that God is rarely recognized by the leaders of the nations, except in a perfunctory way.

God's plan for a man and for a nation is that the glory of God should be central. Our natural man tells us to do all for the glory that is of man. The pride or vainglory of life is the dominating passion with men apart from the grace of God. When we pray, "Lead us not into temptation," we cooperate in answering the prayer by yielding ourselves, body, soul and spirit, to the control of Christ, remembering the word:

"Only one life, 'twill soon be past;

Only what's done for Christ will last."

Chapter 10

But Deliver Us From Evil

If we take this petition, "But deliver us from evil," as a seventh petition in the Lord's Prayer, we recognize its intimate connection with the other petition, "Lead us not into temptation." Deliverance is what we need. Only God has power to give deliverance. He delivers by keeping us free from many testings, and from many temptations to evil. Again, he delivers his children who are not kept free from the testings, but are sorely tried.

The promise that we shall not be tempted above that we are able gives assurance that the Lord chooses our temptations for us. As in the case of Job, he does not permit Satan to go one step beyond God's will. He will not allow a young, untried Christian to meet the testings and temptations that more matured Christians are allowed to undergo. Thus he delivers by keeping us from the testing, or the temptation to evil.

God in his love, however, does not refrain from allowing his children to be overwhelmed with trials, and faced with fearful temptations to evil. Again the promise holds. There is the way of escape, that we may be able to endure the temptation.

Some consider the more accurate rendering: "Deliver us from the evil one." Certainly deliverance from evil will include deliverance from Satan. He has a unique relationship to all evil. Yet the word can be used in the more general sense, and include evil and deceit of every kind. There is evil in our own natures, evil in other men, evil in the world system; these are enemies as well as Satan. There is the triad of evil:

the world, the flesh and the devil.

This petition assures us of the fact that we need fear no evil. We cannot be conquered by any evil circumstance, or by any evil power, because we are in Christ, and we are more than conquerors through him. In the world we are to have tribulation, but we are of good cheer because Christ has overcome the world. Yet for these things he will be enquired of us. Our part is to pray. So we pray, "Deliver us from evil."

We have already noted the remarkable parallel between the twenty-third Psalm, the Psalm of victorious life, and the petitions of the Lord's Prayer.

The Lord is our Shepherd; we shall not lack any good thing. As the shepherd makes the sheep to lie down in green pastures, and leads them beside still waters, so our Shepherd supplies every material need. But we pray, "Give us this day our daily bread."

The Lord is our Shepherd: he restores our soul. We need forgiveness and restoration when we sin; we need encouragement and refreshment when we are overborne. But we pray, "Forgive us our debts, as we forgive our debtors."

The Lord is our Shepherd: he guides us into right paths. But we pray, "Lead us not into temptation."

The Lord is our Shepherd: he delivers us from all fear of evil, and he provides a table before us in the presence of our enemies. But we pray, "Deliver us from evil."

The provision of our Shepherd, meeting every need, is a costly provision indeed. It cost the blood of the Son of God on Calvary. When Christ died, and rose again, and ascended, he sent the gift of the Holy Spirit to abide in the heart of the believer. God makes provision through the Cross of Christ, and through the indwelling power of the Holy Spirit. These blessings belong to every Christian. The Lord is our

Shepherd. That is a fact, not a promise. Yet for all of these things that God has provided he asks us to pray.

In the revelation of the Trinity we have God the Father presented as the source of salvation and of all blessing. All things come from God the Father. Christ Jesus our Lord is presented as the One through whom all blessings come. God the Son is the channel of all blessing. The Holy Spirit is presented as the One who applies to our lives all the benefits purchased by Christ on the cross. The Holy Spirit takes of the things of Christ and makes them real to us. God the Holy Spirit is the agent of all blessings.

God's plan is to give us Christ, and with Christ he freely gives us all things. The Holy Spirit dwelling within takes of these things of Christ and imparts them to us. He takes the joy and peace of Christ, the love and power of Christ, and makes them real in and through us.

What is the place of prayer in this? Though all things come from the Father, by the Son, and through the Spirit, it is true also that all things come in answer to prayer and faith.

As we think of the unspeakable cost of redemption, we realize that the problem God had to deal with was the problem of evil. What a tremendous petition it is then to ask God to deliver us from evil. He has already won the victory. Satan is a conquered foe. Yet the final redemption is not complete, and it has pleased God that we should meet the onslaughts of the enemy. At present he does not set a table before us in the presence of the angels of God. He sets a table before us in the presence of our enemies. As the sheep are surrounded by the enemies that might make their life miserable or destroy them, the lion and the bear, the scorpion and the serpent, so we are surrounded by enemies on every hand. But as David delivered the sheep from the bear and the lion, so our Shepherd delivers us from all the power of the enemy. For this we pray, and we may pray in faith.

There is a yet further meaning in this closing petition, "Deliver us from evil." It is a prophecy of the final victory of Christ over all his and our enemies. It is a prophecy of the time when the kingdoms of this world will become the kingdom of our Lord and of his Christ. It is clearly prophesied that one day there will be a Satan-empowered man called the Antichrist. He will head up all of the anti-Christian system against the things of God. The second Psalm gives a picture of this, when the rulers will take counsel against the Lord God and against his Anointed One saying, "Let us burst their bonds apart." When we pray, "Deliver us from evil," we are praying for the final defeat of Satan, for the hastening of the coming of Christ to reign.

When the Lord told his disciples that men ought always to pray and not to faint, he gave a parable concerning this very matter. He realized that the church would be facing deadly enemies, and at times would be tempted to faint, but the cure for fainting is prayer; and prayer is based on this certainty that the great Enemy will be destroyed. God will bruise Satan under our feet shortly (Rom.16 :20).

This prayer parable is not a general exhortation to perseverance in prayer; it is concerning the widow who said to the judge, "Give me justice against my adversary." So the application is that God directs our crying to him for vengeance against the power of the enemy. The promise is, "he will give justice to them speedily." That is, God's deliverance will not come a moment too late. There follows the solemn word, "Nevertheless, when the Son of Man comes, will he find faith on earth?"

The church is in a conflict. There is no rosy picture of an increasing conquest of the Gospel in this age. There is a sure prophecy of increasing apostasy within the church itself. At the same time God will accomplish his purpose, as in other ages, through a faithful remnant. The answer to the question, "Will he find faith on the earth?" is an affirmative answer. He will find faith. The very question itself, however, precludes the idea of a gradual or rapid bringing of nearly all the world to Christ. In John's day there were many antichrists (1 John 2:18). "The whole world lies in the power of the evil one" (1 John 5:19). On the other hand, there are great and increasing triumphs of the Gospel in winning men out from that wicked world. Thus we have the Bible picture of Satan's program heading up to a climax, and God's program heading up to a climax. Our Lord's parable of the weeds clearly indicates that the wheat and the weeds grow together until the consummation. The truth will not be found in the statement that the world is getting better and better, until it is all controlled by the Gospel, nor on the other hand by the statement that the world is getting worse and worse until the Gospel is extinguished. The light that shines in the darkness will not be overcome or conquered by the darkness. But God will be inquired of for this consummation. One of the means he uses for the victory is the prayers of his people. The Church has prayed, "Deliver us from evil," or "Deliver us from the evil one," and this prayer will be answered finally when Satan and all his hosts are cast into the lake of fire.

When men take Christ as Saviour they turn unto God from idols "to serve the living and true God, and to wait for his Son from heaven, whom he raised from the dead, Jesus who delivers us from the wrath to come" (1 Thess. 1: 9, 10). God in his grace has postponed the wrath that is to be poured out upon the world. Christians will need to be delivered from that wrath. This is the great future of our redemption. True believers will persevere to the end, but it is a real perseverance, and no superficial idea that Christians will be given victory no matter what they do. We are to pray, "Deliver us from evil," and that prayer has its consummation at the completion of our salvation, the redemption of the body, when our union with Christ will be complete.

Thus there is an individual fulfillment of this petition, first in present victory over our enemies, finally in our complete perfection in Christ. There is the other fulfillment in the completion of God's purposes for the universe. This will be in two great stages in the future: first, when Christ returns again to reign with his saints, and, finally, when he delivers up the kingdom to the Father, and there will begin what we call the eternal state.

The Lord's Prayer, then, does not break off abruptly, but covers all things that are needful for this life and for eternity.

The doxology that concludes the Lord's prayer, "For yours is the kingdom and the power and the glory," would seem to rise spontaneously from the believer's heart. These words are omitted in many modern versions, and the judgment of most scholars is that they were added later to the prayer, probably in the first century. However, other scholars would regard them as words used by the Lord Jesus himself. The prayer fittingly concludes with praise and worship and adoration, and also with a triumphant note of faith in recognizing that prayer will be answered, and that the kingdom and the power and the glory will forever be ascribed to God our Saviour.

The "Amen" is a final word of assurance, taking away all hesitancy. It is a note of thanksgiving for the sure answer.

Chapter 11

The Final Secret of Prayer

The disciple's request, "Lord, teach us to pray," was answered in the matchless words of the Lord's Prayer. However, this was not all of the answer. There follows in the eleventh chapter of Luke the vivid parable of the importunate friend, and after that several parable-similes to press home the truth of prevailing prayer.

The Lord gives the parable of the three friends. Someone has spoken of these as the needy friend, the mighty friend, and the praying friend. The man who has nothing to set before his friend goes to his neighbor with a very definite request. He needs three loaves. The friend does not want to be disturbed. If he rises his whole household will be wakened. But the friend has come to get the three loaves, and he is not going to leave until his request is granted. It is soon apparent to the friend who has the bread that his household will be disturbed in any case, and he rises and gives him the thing that he asks for.

We are not to take from this parable that God is unwilling to bless, like the man in the parable, but that he will respond to coaxing. The one point of the parable is that his earthly friend answered the request because of the importunity of the petitioner. Even more so will God answer the prayers of his children who will not be denied.

The Lord presses this truth home by a series of three proverbial sayings: "Ask, and it will be given to you; seek, and you will find; knock, and it will be opened to you." Here is a principle that is true in life generally. Our Lord is applying it to prayer: "For everyone who asks receives, and the one who seeks finds, and to the one who knocks it will be opened." They who receive are they who ask, and they who find are they who seek, and they who have doors opened are they who knock on the doors. The Lord then gives the illustration of the earthly fathers who give to their children good gifts when they ask. All the more will the heavenly Father give good things to those who ask him.

The same teaching is given in the Sermon on the Mount, and is followed by the words: "If you then, who are evil, know how to give good gifts to your children, how much more will your Father who is in heaven give good things to those who ask him!" (Matt. 7:11). In Luke there is a significant change. The question is put, "How much more will your Father who is in heaven give the Holy Spirit to those who ask him?" It is not a different teaching. God gives all things to Christ. He gives Christ to us when we accept him, and with Christ he freely gives us all things. He gives the gift of the Holy Spirit, and the work of the Holy Spirit to take of the things of Christ and make them real to us. Thus all good things are comprehended in the prayer for the Holy Spirit.

Some judge that this prayer for the Holy Spirit was for the disciples before Pentecost. Every Christian today has the Holy Spirit dwelling within him or her (Rom. 8:9; 1 Cor. 3:16, 6:19). But this is not intended as a prayer for believers to ask for the gift of the Holy Spirit, which came at Pentecost; the primary meaning of this prayer for the Holy Spirit is for all the things that come to us through the Holy Spirit. The name of the Holy Spirit is used to include all of those things that the Holy Spirit gives. But God gives them in answer to prayer: "Some prayer, some blessing. More prayer, more blessing. Much prayer, much blessing."

The central truth in all of these prayer teachings which follow the Lord's Prayer, is that there is no such thing as an unanswered prayer.

We are to pray in faith, and to keep on praying till the answer comes.

It is true that many of our petitions may be denied. Paul sought the Lord Christ three times and did not have his request granted. But who will say that Paul's prayer was not answered? He himself rejoiced in an answer far beyond the definite thing he had requested. Are we then to be satisfied to pray, and to consider that the prayer is answered when we do not receive what we ask for? Are we to conclude that in every case the reason for the lack of answer to prayer is the fact that it is not God's will to grant that request? This is by no means true. There are conditions to prevailing prayer. The conditions have already been suggested in our study of the Lord's Prayer. We are to abide in Christ, and his words are to abide in us. When we delight ourselves in the Lord, the desires of our hearts are for his glory, and he grants those desires. We are to come with worship in our hearts, with confession of sins, and with forgiveness in our hearts toward others. All of these are vital conditions. The reason for unanswered prayer is the failure to meet definite conditions laid down in God's Word.

There is the condition of persistence in prayer, praying until the answer comes. There is the condition of following our Lord's practice in regular times of prayer. The observance of the quiet time is one of the most necessary habits to insure a successful prayer life. We should set our faces like a flint to get this prayer time in the morning, if at all possible; before we meet other people we should meet God. In the quiet time there should be first the feeding on his Word. After lifting our hearts in prayer to God to give a message, we should come for that devotional study and receive a personal message from the Word. With that as a background, we then come in prayer as he taught us to pray.

There are many consecrated Christians who are faithful in observing all of these conditions, yet they are disappointed in the results of their prayer life. It is probably true that the greatest reason for the failure to get answers to prayer on the part of consecrated Christians is lack of faith.

We may be startled into this truth concerning prayer if we put it this way: it is because Christians pray, "If it is your will," that they fail to get answers to their prayers. It sounds like a shocking statement; are we not always to pray, "If it is your will?" That certainly is ever to be the spirit of our approach to God; but consider what it would mean if we are to use this "if" in every petition. It would mean that we can never be assured of what the will of God is. It would mean that we always put upon God the responsibility of answered prayer. But the Lord Jesus again and again puts the responsibility for answered prayer up to his disciples (Mark 11:22-24; John 14:13-14; 15:7, 16; 16:23-24).

The Father is more eager to reveal his will to his children than an earthly father is. Here is a child who comes to the father and says he is so grateful for all the father and mother have done for him that he has decided to do everything just the way his father and mother want him to do it. Can we suppose that there is a father who would tell such a son that he is not ever going to tell him what his will is? He must go and do the best he can, and decide himself whether he is pleasing the father or not. While we smile at such a thought, is this not the way that we regard the heavenly Father? We consider his will a mystery. It is true that in many things we do not know God's will; then we should pray, "If it is your will," and have the patience of committing the whole matter to him. But in multiplied cases it is God's pleasure to reveal his will. Then we are to pray without any "if" — we are to pray in faith.

There is, of course, the danger of presumption. There is the danger of a false ground for prayer, as when Christians are exhorted to pray for bodily healing and then to claim that bodily healing on the authority of God's Word. If there is real faith, there will be healing, but to claim healing, or to claim other blessings, on a wrong interpretation of God's Word is not to pray in faith, but in presumption or at least in ignorance.

What is the meaning of this startling word: "Have faith in God. Truly, I say to you, whoever says to this mountain, 'Be taken up and thrown into the sea,' and does not doubt in his heart, but believes that what he says will come to pass, it will be done for him. Therefore I tell you, whatever you ask in prayer, believe that you have received it, and it will be yours." (Mark 11:22-24)?

The final secret for answered prayer is to pray in faith. Thank God for the answer. We are not infallible. We need to come with humble, contrite hearts, often trembling and not sure that this or that is God's will. But this is the glorious promise that we by persistence may discover what God's will is. As we persevere, he reveals in one way or another that he desires to hear our prayer. Let us then believe that we have the petition we desired of him.

There is nothing too great for God's power. There is nothing too small for God's love. There is nothing, therefore, outside the realm of prayer.

Two ministers were talking with loved ones at the bedside of a dying man. The pastor of the man was telling of God's wonderful answers to prayer in healing. However, he did not feel that he could pray the prayer of faith for a miracle in the case of this brother. It appeared that this was God's time for him to go. When the pastor told of another remarkable answer to prayer for healing of the husband of one of the friends who was present, the other minister exclaimed, "Prayer changes things!" Then the pastor told of this incident:

"I have in my office one of those mottoes, 'Prayer changes things.' One day I came to my office and found that my new secretary had mislaid the combination of the safe. All my papers were in the safe, and important things needed to be done. I sat for a moment in prayer wondering what to do. I raised my head and saw this motto: 'Prayer changes things.' I exclaimed, 'It certainly does.' I arose and turned the motto, and on the back was the combination to the safe. I had written it there a year or more before, in case it should be mislaid."

Yes, it is true. The combination to every locked safe is prayer. God is the one who changes things. He is the one who works mighty works. There is nothing too hard for him. He has given us the keys to unlock every door. He has given us the combination to every safe. Let us use it, and let us add faith to our prayers, for the heart of real prayer is faith.

About the Author

Robert C. McQuilkin (1886–1952) was the first president of Columbia International University from 1923-1952. In 1918, McQuilkin and his wife Marguerite were days away from an assignment as missionaries when the ship that was to carry them to Africa burned and sunk the day before the ship's departure. That left McQuilkin questioning God's next move for him and opened up the opportunity for McQuilkin to later accept the position to lead a new work in Columbia, South Carolina, called the Southern Bible Institute. It would soon be renamed Columbia Bible College, and by 1994, Columbia International University.

After earning a bachelor's degree from the University of Pennsylvania, McQuilkin began working in 1912 as associate editor for the influential *Sunday School Times*. It was during this period that McQuilkin established the Oxford Conference in Pennsylvania where he proclaimed the "Victorious Christian Life" message, which would become a core value of CIU.

In conjunction with CIU, McQuilkin founded the Ben Lippen Conference Center, a place where the Victorious Christian Life was proclaimed and where young people were encouraged to consider the mission field.

During his ministry, McQuilkin spoke widely and authored a number of books including, *The Lord is My Shepherd, Let Not Your Heart be Troubled, Victory in Christ,* and *Joy and Victory.*

CIU | Columbia
International
University

Columbia International University exists to train men and women from a biblical world view to impact the nations with the message of Christ through service in the marketplace, missions and the local church.

For more information about undergraduate, graduate and seminary programs at Columbia International University, visit www.ciu.edu

Scan this QR code with a smartphone
to visit www.ciu.edu